The Our Father
Four Commentaries on The Lord's Prayer

Written and Compiled by
Fr. Bill McCarthy, MSA

The Our Father – *Four Commentaries on The Lord's Prayer*

Copyright © 1999 St. Andrew's Productions
ISBN: 1-891903-15-2
All Rights Reserved

St. Andrew's Productions
6111 Steubenville Pike
McKees Rocks, PA 15136

Phone: (412) 787-9735
Fax: (412) 787-5204
Website: www.SaintAndrew.com

The Publisher gratefully acknowledges use of the following materials:

The Lord's Prayer by St. Thomas Aquinas, excerpted from **The Three Greatest Prayers**, published by Sophia Institute Press, Manchester, New Hampshire, copyright 1990. Printed with permission.

The Lord's Prayer: "Our Father!", excerpted from the **Catechism of the Catholic Church**, Part Four, Section Two, English translation for the United States of America copyright 1994, United States Catholic Conference, Inc. – Liberia Editrice Vaticana. Printed with permission.

A Treatise on the Lord's Prayer by Saint Cyprian, Bishop and Martyr. The MIGNE text, PLU, 519-544 is entirely superceded by the Edition of W. Hartel in CSEL Vol. 3, Part 1, Vienna, 1868, pp. 265-294.

Table of Contents

CHAPTER III
A TREATISE ON THE LORD'S PRAYER
by Saint Cyprian, Bishop and Martyr 71

Fr. Bill McCarthy with Pope John Paul II, Rome, 1995

Fr. Bill is co-director and co-founder of *My Father's House*, a spiritual retreat center in Moodus, Connecticut. Ordained in Rome, he is a Scripture scholar and is a member of the *Holy Apostles Community* in Cromwell. Fr. Bill devotes his time to giving retreats, counseling, spiritual direction, and teaching, as well as giving parish missions and addressing conferences in Connecticut and throughout the country.

Preface

This is not simply another book about prayer. It's about *THE* prayer of all prayers — the *Our Father*. It also is not simply an exposition on the *Our Father*, but rather four different meditations or commentaries on the way to pray that Jesus taught us. One of the commentaries was written by St. Cyprian in the 3RD Century, one of them was written by St. Thomas Aquinas in the 13TH Century, and the other two meditations or expositions were written in the 20TH Century — one by a priest and one by the Church Universal. Looking at the *Our Father* through four different perspectives brings some of the height, depth, length and breadth of a Catholic perspective.

Why This Book?

Each of us struggles with prayer. Part of the struggle is that we do not know how to pray. Another part of the struggle is that there are so many ways to pray that we get confused as to which one is the best. But the way above all ways to pray is that which Jesus taught us by His example — an example that is also reflected in the wisdom tradition of the Catholic Church.

This is a simple book but a life-changing one. If you listen well to what is written here for you, then neither your prayer life nor, for that matter, your life as a whole, will ever be the same again.

As you begin to follow the life-changing petitions and principles that Jesus taught us, a new energy will explode into your life. By following His admonition to praise and worship God... by learning how to listen as He reveals His Will... by depending upon His Father to provide for your daily needs... by receiving and giving love and forgiveness... and by walking under the protective hand of God, you will become more childlike and, thus, more Christ-like, as well.

Each of the saints, in their own way, has discovered how prayer changes things, and how the *Lord's Prayer* changes EVERYTHING.

> Teresa of Avila could not utter the words "Our Father"
> without going into a slight ecstasy.

Charles Peguy, in his powerful "Vision of Prayer", reveals his personal conversion noting: "Our Father who art in heaven," — those three or four words that conquered me the unconquerable.

St. Augustine states, "The daily prayer, which Jesus Himself taught and for which reason it is called the Lord's Prayer, certainly takes away daily sins when we say daily, 'Forgive us our trespasses.'"

The Didiche, one of the early Christian writings on the Church, advises, "Do not pray as the hypocrites do, but as the Lord commanded in his Gospel: you shall pray thus, pray the Our Father three times a day."

St. Cyril of Jerusalem states, "We say that prayer that the Savior imparted to his own disciples and with a pure conscience, we describe God as Father. Oh how great is the loving kindness of God."

St. Caesar of Arles says, "Know the Creed and the Lord's Prayer yourselves and teach them to your children. I do not know how a man can call himself a Christian by signing his forehead when he neglects to learn the few short lines of the Creed or the Lord's Prayer."

Pope Paul VI said that for all the prayer that he had ever learned, the one he prayed over and over again was the *Our Father*. By the time he neared the end of his life, he revealed that he only prayed the first half because it was the only part that was meaningful. But in the last two days of his life, he said that the one word that meant anything to him any more was "Father"; and he repeated the words, "Father, Abba, Father, Abba" as he died.

What really prompted this book, however, was an experience I had six years ago when the Lord taught me the difference between **saying** the *Our Father* and **praying** the *Our Father*. In the Our Father are life-changing principles that if followed will open up the human heart to the treasures of God's love and unseal for us the treasury of graces.

Like the saints who attained union with God after persistency in prayer, expect to be challenged, expect to be changed, expect to grow in your intimacy with Christ and the Father, expect to enter more deeply into a personal relationship with Christ who says, "He who sees me, sees the Father." By praying the *Our Father*, expect to be filled with the Spirit of the Father and the Son, a spirit of childlike trust and dependency, a spirit of hope and a spirit of love.

My Conversion: A Personal, Intimate Relationship With Christ

Two decades ago, at a downpoint in my priesthood, I made a retreat with a priest who had a personal relationship with Jesus. I asked him how this precious relationship and his prayerlife with Jesus had developed. And he told me the most profound story that dramatically changed my life.

He explained that after a downpoint in his priesthood, he decided to isolate himself in a cave in Spain that had a reputation for being a very holy place. For nine months, he stayed alone by himself in that cave with one purpose — to seek a deeper intimacy with God. He had made arrangements for an old man to bring him only bread and water and oil for his lamp. And, there in the cave, 7,000 feet above sea level, he shut himself off alone with God, not knowing what to expect.

As he entered the cave, all he knew of prayer was what most of us had been taught — that prayer is one-sided — a one-way street for us to talk to God. So in the beginning weeks, he cried out to God through his loneliness, his fear, his guilt and even his disbelief. "My God", he thought, "I'm not even too sure you are there."

Finally, at the end of his crying out to God, he got very, very quiet. In his own silence, with nothing to turn on and no one to talk to, he became totally aware of his complete solitude and aloneness. And then it happened. A new stream of thoughts came clearly into his mind. He heard the words, "Brennan, I love you, and I called you here to be alone with Me. And even though you're passing through many fiery temptations, you shall not be burned. And though you are overwhelmed with many worries and fears, you shall not be drowned. For you are precious in My eyes and honored. I forbid you to be afraid."

At the end of the stream of thoughts a page number from his Bible came clearly into his mind. With great anticipation, he opened his Bible to that page; and there, to his utter amazement, he read these words from the 43rd chapter of Isaiah, the Prophet: "I love you, I call you by your name, you are Mine. Though you pass through the fires, you shall not be burned. Though you pass through the waters you shall not drown. For you are precious in My eyes and honored. I forbid you to be afraid."

Then and there, he realized two simple truths: first, that Jesus Christ was alive and well and living in his own heart; and second, that this Jesus was speaking to him from within his own thoughts. He could talk to Christ, then he would listen, and Christ would talk back to him. He developed a very intimate, personal relationship with the God who lived in his heart.

One day in prayer, the Lord took him into an ecstasy and in that ecstatic state, God said to him through his own thoughts, "You are My beloved son upon whom my favor rests. I'm going to use you very simply, lovingly and powerfully among my people. And finally, after nine glorious months alone with Christ, the Lord sent him forth with a very simple, but powerful message:

> The Lord said, "Go and tell every single person that you meet that I love them with my whole heart and my whole soul. I love them regardless of their weaknesses and their sins. I love them and I want to be Lord of their hearts. And if they surrender their poor battered hearts to me, I promise that whatever they ask the Father in My Name I will give to them. And the miracles that I've done before I shall begin to do in their own lives."

After hearing this powerful story from this very simple, loving priest, I left my retreat changed forever. For I realized that a deep, personal, intimate prayerlife is the sole foundation for a deep, personal intimate relationship with God. The same is true for you. God is with you now as you read these words. In fact, He is constantly at your side, leading you, guiding you, whispering in your ear and tugging at your heart as you read these pages. So, resolve to remain open to His promptings as you read through the pages of this book.

My Prayer For You

It is in this intimate, interpersonal way that this book is meant to be read so that each of you may come to know the love, the protection, the peace, the healing and the providential guidance of an all-loving Father made manifest in Jesus through the power of the Spirit. As you listen to the Father, may you love with the Son and live in that Spirit. And may the Spirit of the Father and the Son fill your mind with Their Wisdom, inflame your heart with Their Love and empower your life with Their Spirit.

Fr. Bill McCarthy, MSA
Easter Sunday, 1998

INTRODUCTION TO PRAYER

by Fr. Bill McCarthy, MSA

"**P**ray Without Ceasing"

Prayer is not simply talking to God; it is communicating with Him — having a heart-to-heart conversation with God. Prayer is a two-way street; we talk to Him, He talks to us. It is an intimate time for us to come into union with God. Therefore, a life of prayer comprises the habit of entering into and being in the presence of God who loves us — of being in communion with Him.

That is what St. Paul meant when he said, "pray without ceasing." Every moment is an opportunity to be in union with God. That is why we must learn to talk AND to listen to Him. We need to take time to learn the ways in which God speaks to us and what His voice sounds like.

But even though communication with God is a two-way street, prayer is not a question of equal time. The person with the most important message should have more time. So, it goes without saying that God's message is far more important than anything we have to say to Him. Consequently, in prayer, we should spend more time listening to Him than speaking. With Samuel, we pray: "Speak, Lord, for Your servant is listening" (1 Sam 3:10).

There are many methods of prayer and many ways to express prayer — vocal, mental, liturgical, devotional, spontaneous, private, shared, meditative, contemplative, even tears, laughter, painting, singing, dancing, giving, and the circumstances of life itself. Moreover, there are several forms of prayer — praise, thanksgiving, blessing, adoration, petition, and intercession

Yet, the one prayer that rises above all others as the most perfect of prayers is the *Lord's Prayer*. Why? Because it was taught by the master and model pray-er, the Lord Jesus Himself.

This book provides four powerful commentaries or meditations on the *Lord's Prayer*. It serves to illuminate this quintessential prayer of the Church that stands at the center of the Scriptures. For as the

Church father, Tertullian, observed, it summarizes the whole gospel.

We can take our example from "people of prayer" in Scripture: Moses, whose face reflected God's glory (cf Ex. 34: 33,35); Mary, who listened and did the will of the Father (Lk 1:26-38); and Jesus, who taught that the message of prayer is that of a life lived abundantly — one that is lived in relationship with the Source of Life, the Father. Ultimately, the essence of Jesus' prayer is Jesus saying "Yes" to the still voice of the Father and then doing only what the Father tells Him to do. That is our goal, as well — to live out of the Father, in union with His Will.

The examples of these holy Biblical people teach us that prayer is learning to always *listen* to God talk to us. If we faithfully ask God to speak to us and reveal His Kingdom and His Will, He will! "Ask and you shall receive" is a promise. When we really seek God's Kingdom and Will with all our heart, we will find Him. Thus, we can continually flow out of God by listening to His voice spoken in the present moment.

This truth is captured in the following insight offered by Mother Teresa of Calcutta on the importance of prayer.

> *It is not possible to engage in the direct apostolate without being a soul of prayer. We must be aware of oneness with Christ as He was aware of oneness with His Father. Our activity is truly apostolic only in so far as we permit Him to work in us and through us, with His power, with His desire, with His love. We must become holy, not because we want to feel holy, but because Christ must be able to live His life fully in us. We are to be all love, all faith, all purity for the sake of the poor we serve. And once we have learned to seek God and His will, our contacts with the poor will become the means of great sanctity to ourselves and to others.*
>
> *Therefore, love to pray. Feel often during the day the need for prayer and take trouble to pray. For prayer enlarges the heart until it is capable of containing God's gift of Himself. Ask and seek, and your heart will grow big enough to receive Him and keep Him as your own.*

Each of us is called to holiness — true union with God in both mind and heart. Our highest purpose is to give glory to God, and the vehicle for that is prayer. We were made to enjoy God and to find joy in Him. Prayer leads us to a sense of self-worth and inner happiness that enables us to live a life of loving union with God and selfless service of our neighbor. Bishop Fulton Sheen, who spent three hours in prayer daily, understood that fully. He knew that prayer went to the core of a satisfying, joy-filled and sanctified life.

Our Assurance in Prayer:
God is more willing to hear us than we are to ask.

"Ask and it will be given to you; seek and you will find; knock and the door will be opened to you. For everyone who asks receives; he who seeks finds; and to him who knocks, the door will be opened" (Mt 7:7-8).

In this section of the Sermon on the Mount, Jesus assures us that our prayers will be heard and answered. We notice that Jesus uses words which mean almost the same thing, and each time He mentions that, He repeats the promise of assurance that our prayers being heard and answered.

He tells us to ask, and He promises us that we shall receive.

He tells us to seek, and promises that we will find.

He tells us to knock, and He promises us that doors will be opened.

Thus, by repeating the asking, seeking and knocking of the person praying, He impresses deep into our minds this one truth — that we may confidently expect answers to our prayers.

Next, to the revelation of the Father's love, there is in the whole course of the school of prayer, no more important method than this: that EVERYONE WHO ASKS SHALL RECEIVE.

The Lord uses three words — ask, seek and knock in teaching us how to pray effectively — ASK for the gifts we pray for… SEEK the presence of the giver… and KNOCK to open the door that leads to our enjoyment of the Father's love and guidance.

Jesus wants us to realize without any doubt that our asking, seeking and knocking simply cannot be in vain. The assured fruit of prayer is in receiving an answer, finding God and opening up our hearts to do the Father's Will. The Lord knows how doubt and mistrust toward God are so natural to us. He understands how easily we are inclined to rest in prayer as a religious principle without receiving an answer. He understands also that even when we have faith that God will hear our prayer, true faith-filled prayer is something too high and difficult for the half-hearted person.

Therefore, at the very beginning of his teaching on prayer, Jesus seeks to impart this thought deep into our hearts: PRAYER DOES AVAIL MUCH. Ask and you shall receive is a fixed and eternal law of the Kingdom of God. Everyone who asks shall receive. Jesus assures us that if we have prayed fervently and sincerely, we will receive an answer.

According to Jesus, prayer consists of two parts, our part and God's part. Our part is the asking, seeking and knocking; God's part is the giving, revealing and the opening. Our part is to ask; God's part is to make sure we receive. Our part is to seek; God's part is to make sure we find. Our part is to knock; God's part is to open the doors.

The Our Father:
The Way Above All Ways

Many Christians today do not pray with the faith, the fervor and the fidelity that enable us to seize the very promises of God. Our Heavenly Father seeks daily fellowship with all of His children so that He can listen to and grant our requests. He wills that you and I should come to Him day by day with distinct and personal requests. He wills day by day to do for us what we ask. It was through His answer to prayer that the saints of old learned how to know God as the Living One who constantly intervened in their lives.

Surprisingly, people find it difficult to grasp that God is that close to us, that He really wants an ongoing, intimate, personal relationship with us in which He hears our prayers and answers them. Therefore, we need to reach out in trust and seek at all times this divine and practical truth. Our prayer on earth and God's answer from heaven are two sides of the same coin. As we ask, we receive. As we seek, we find. As we knock, doors will be opened for us.

It is my hope that in the following pages you will come to understand what it means to truly *pray* the *Lord's Prayer*. It is my prayer that you surrender and humbly ask the Lord to teach you to pray with assurance and with faith.

THE LORD'S PRAYER
by Fr. Bill McCarthy, MSA

t some point along our faith journey, each of us has stopped to ask, "Is there a specific and special way to pray?" The Catholic Christian tradition is so rich that there really is no one, specific way to pray. Some people prefer the rosary. Some people call upon the intercession of St. Jude. Others find meaning in liturgical prayer, while some people repeat the Jesus prayer. But, Jesus Christ, Himself, revealed a prayer that is simple, easy to know, and that is the way above all ways to pray — the Pater Noster or, as we know it, the *Lord's Prayer*.

Lord, Teach Us To Pray – The Lord's Prayer
At one time, Jesus was praying and when He had finished, one of His disciples came to Him with this request, "Lord, teach us to pray as John taught his disciples" (Lk 11:1). And Jesus said to His disciples, "After this manner pray, "'Our Father in heaven, hallowed be your name, your kingdom come, your will be done on earth as it is in heaven. Give us today our daily bread. Forgive us our debts, as we also have forgiven our debtors. And lead us not into temptation, but deliver us from the evil one'" (Mt 6:9-13).

In order to fully understand the importance of Jesus' answer, let us first look at the request, *Lord teach us to pray*.

Lord
The disciple is addressing Jesus who IS prayer and the master of prayer. Jesus is the Lord of prayer. The disciple is not asking one of the apostles or a teacher or a head rabbi. He is addressing his request to the very Son of God, the very wisdom of God, the one who knows the Father intimately. He is addressing himself to the great master and teacher of all spirituality, but especially the teacher of prayer. He is asking God the Incarnate, Himself, to teach him and others how to pray.

Teach

The disciple is asking the Lord to teach him and others how to pray, expecting that Jesus will show him the way and the steps to prayer. He is trusting that the Lord will show him the prerequisites of prayer, the purposes of prayer, the correct attitudes of prayer, and the power of prayer. The disciple is asking for a divine blueprint which will encompass practical steps that can be studied and learned.

Us

The request of the disciple is not just a personal one; he wants to learn how to pray, not only for himself but also for others. The disciple is obviously not a self-centered person. And from his requests, one can discern that most likely, in learning to pray himself, he in turn will teach others.

To Pray

This is the key concept here. The disciple is not asking the Lord to give him a formula or ritual that he can recite. The disciple is not asking Him for a list of words that he can memorize. The disciple is asking Jesus to enter into the intimate, powerful, exchange of conversation with God. The disciple is asking Jesus to teach Him to PRAY.

I emphasize this because most people do not understand the power and the practicality of Jesus' response. The reason is because they misinterpret the word *pray* that is requested by the disciple. It's not uncommon for most of us to think to ourselves, "Hey, I say the *Our Father*. I even know it by heart." But that's the problem. We **say** the "*Our Father*"; we don't **pray** the "*Our Father*". There are millions of Christians who SAY the "*Our Father*". There are precious few who PRAY it.

After this Manner Pray

Jesus, having heard the request of the disciple, gives us the way above all ways to pray. He says in effect, "This is how to pray;" that is, after this manner, pray. What follows are not simply words or empty formulas or cold rituals, but *three powerful insights*. The first insight concerns our nature. The second insight is into the nature of God. And the third insight contains five life-changing, practical principles of effective and efficacious prayer.

The Three Insights – OUR FATHER

The *first insight* is that we are actually praying to *Our* Father.

We are not simply praying to the man upstairs or to the Creator of the universe, but to our all-loving, all-merciful Father. In order to remove all doubt and to show us on what sure ground the principles rest, God appeals to everyone at an intimate level of our lived experience — that is, the relationship we have with our own father.

Each of us has a father; and nothing is as natural to a father than answering the request of his child. The Lord asks us to look first to our earthly father and then to His Father. "For what man is there among you whom if his son asks for bread will give him a stone? Or if he asks him for a fish will give him a serpent? If you, being evil then, know how to give good gifts to your children, how much more shall your Father who is in heaven give good things to them that ask for them" (Mt 7:9-11).

As simple and as intelligible as this truth is, deep and spiritual is the teaching it contains. Jesus is reminding us that the prayer of a child owes its influence entirely to the relation in which he stands to his father. The power of the promise, *ask and it shall be given to you*, lies in the relationship between us as children with the Father in heaven. When we live and walk in that relationship, the prayer of faith and childlike simplicity will have a natural result.

We have to become children before God, trusting Him with childlike simplicity to watch over us and to care for our needs; to protect us and help us day by day; to feed us and clothe us as our needs may be; to forgive us and love us so that we may be happy.

St. Paul tells us that those who are led by the Spirit of God are children of God. The childlike privilege of asking for everything is inseparable from the childlike life of the leading of the Holy Spirit. The people who allow themselves to be led by the Spirit in their lives will be lead by the Spirit in their prayers, as well. They will find that *father-like giving is God's response to childlike living.*

Over and again, Jesus stresses these two realities: first that God is our Father, and second, that we are His children. In the Beatitudes, for example, Jesus teaches that those of childlike purity and poverty shall be called, "Children of God" (Mt 5:3-9). Moreover, they are the children who let their light shine before men so that they may glorify their Father in heaven; who walk in love, "that you may be the children of your Father who is in heaven," and who seek to be perfect "even as your Father who is in heaven is perfect" (cf Mt 5:45,48).

Picture the best earthly father that you know. Meditate on the tenderness and love with which he regards the requests of his children. Picture the love and joy with which he grants every reasonable desire. Then consider how much more tenderness and joy our Heavenly Father feels when we come to Him with our honest and sincere requests. The Father wants us to come and open our hearts to Him.

Before we make our way through the five principles or petitions of prayer, we must humbly cleanse our hearts of certain false images drawn from the world. As the *Catechism of the Catholic Church* states: "Humility makes us recognize that no one knows the Son except the Father, and no one knows the Father except the Son and anyone to whom the Son chooses to reveal him, that is, to little children."

Our

The second insight is that this Father is the Father of us all. He is Our Father; we do not stand alone. No man is an island. We work together, we worship together, we pray together, and we receive together. My Father is your Father. He is Our Father. Therefore, prayer is personal but also at the same time altruistic, i.e., my concerns include your concerns; my requests include your requests.

Who Art in Heaven

This biblical expression does not mean a place; nor does it mean that God is distant but majestic — the *third insight*. God transcends every place. As St. Augustine says, "'Our Father who art in heaven' is rightly understood to mean that God is in the hearts of the just as in His holy temple. At the same time, it means that those who pray should desire the one they invoke to dwell in them." And as St. Cyril of Jerusalem says, "Heaven could also be those who bear the image of the heavenly world and in whom God dwells."

The symbol of the heavens refers us back to the mystery of the covenant. God is in heaven and the Father's house is our homeland. Sin and selfishness exile us from the land of the covenant; but conversion of heart enables us to return to the very Holy of Holies, the dwelling place of God. In Christ, heaven and earth are reconciled.

When the Church prays, "Our Father who art in heaven," she is professing that we are the people of God already seated with Him in "the heavenly realms of Jesus" (Eph 2:6); and already "hidden with Christ in God" (Col 3:3). Our Father's house is the true homeland in which we live and dwell and have our being. His rule and His kingdom are not only among us, they are within us. The Spirit of the Father and the Son indwelling our spirits transports us to God's Kingdom and brings heaven to earth.

Praying the "Our Father"

Using the wealth of our spiritual tradition, there are seven petitions found in the *Our Father*. These petitions are presented here as the five "P's" or principles that will serve as guideposts along our prayer journey. (See Appendix A.) The use of these petitions or principles can transform us into *other Christs*, and can transform our daily prayer time from a chore into a delight. The first half of the *Our Father* concerns us and our needs.

FIRST PRINCIPLE or Petition:
Praise: "Hallowed Be Thy Name"

The first thing that Jesus taught us was PRAISE: *Our Father, hallowed be Thy name*. Praising God takes us out of self and puts us into God. Spirituality is not so much inviting God into our little and picayune hearts as it is accepting God's invitation to go up into His heart that has a length, breadth, height and depth that is beyond anything we can think of or imagine. Praise frees up everything within us. When we praise God, such as by saying:

Oh God, You are
>   so holy - all holy
>   so wonderful - all wonderful

so loving - all loving
so merciful - all merciful
so majestic - all majestic
so powerful - all powerful,

then we forget ourselves. The song, *We Have Come Into His House*, says it best. "So forget about yourself and concentrate on Him and worship Him."

In the fourth chapter of John's gospel, Jesus tells the woman at the well that the Father is seeking those who can worship Him in spirit and in truth. In I Colossians, 3:17, Paul gives the principle, "Whatever you do, whether in word or deed, do it all in the name of the Lord Jesus, giving thanks to the Father through Him." We are here to give honor and glory to God our Father.

In the new Catechism, there is a beautiful scene painted by St. John in the book of Revelation. He pictures the Father on the throne with Christ the Lamb, who had been slain, by his right side; surrounded by all the saints, most primarily His mother and all the angels; and finally, "a great multitude, which no one can number, from every nation, tribe, people and tongue." Then it states, "It is into this eternal liturgy that the Spirit and the Church enables us to participate whenever we celebrate the mystery of salvation in the sacraments.

What a beautiful thought that our worship and praise penetrates into the throne room of God where, in union with the saints and angels from Adam to the last saint who has entered into heaven this day, are adoring , praising and worshipping God, Father, Son and Spirit, singing, "Holy, Holy, Holy be the Lord God of Hosts."

Whenever St. Therese, the Little Flower, got bogged down with her problems and would cry out to the Father, He would take her in Spirit into His loving arms and from this high vantage point she would look down on her now little problems and wonder how she ever could have worried about them at all. Praise links us to God, separating us from ego. Praise stirs up the Spirit within us. Praise lifts us out of selfishness, worry and fear. Praise can lead us spiritually, emotionally, and even physically away from ourselves and toward God. Read St. Augustine's insight on the power and importance of praise.

"Our thoughts in this present life should turn on the praise of God, because it is in praising God that we shall rejoice forever in the life to come; and no one can be ready for the next life unless he trains himself for it now.

We are praising God now, assembled as we are here in church; but when we go our various ways again, it seems as if we cease to praise God. But provided we do not cease to live a good life, we shall always be praising God. You cease to praise God only when you swerve from justice and from what is pleasing to God. If you never turn aside from the good life, your tongue may be silent but your actions will cry aloud, and God will perceive your intentions; for as our ears hear each other's voices, so do God's ears hear our thoughts."

~ St. Augustine on Praise

We praise God as Our Father. What a beautiful realization that the God who made the heavens and earth wishes to be called Our Father. Thus, we can worship Him as Father — the one who gives life, the one who loves us unconditionally, the one who is covenanted to provide for our needs, the one who feeds us and protects us, our Abba (cf. Ps 91:12; Is 32:1; 41:1-3; Ps 23:1-4; Ps 100; Ps 36; Ps 145).

Praise God As Our Father, Our Abba

The most celebrated picture of God as Father is found in Luke 15:11-32, in the story of the father of the prodigal son, who is never more of a father than when he welcomes home (back into the family) the one who by his words and deeds has brought shame upon himself and has caused sorrow and pain to those who truly love him. The phrase, *Our Father*, not only introduces the *Lord's Prayer*, but it is also the dominant theme of it, just as in the story of the prodigal son. To get a sense of this, gently repeat the *Abba Prayer* as a means of tapping into a spirit of praise and meditation.

Abba Prayer
Abba, I adore You.
    Abba, I adore You.
        Abba, I adore You.
            Abba, my Abba.

As Father God is a living, thinking, loving being (cf. Acts 17:24-29; 1 Tm 6:15-16; 1 Tm 1:17). He is more than just a divine Mind, or Creator, or First Cause; He is a loving, caring Father. Praising Him opens our spirits to all that He has in store for us.

A Prayer of Awe
You, O eternal Trinity, are a deep sea into which,
the more I enter, the more I find, and the more I find,
the more I seek.
    O abyss,
        O eternal Godhead,
            O sea profound,
what more could You give me than Yourself? Amen.
          ~ Catherine of Siena

So the first part of our prayer time should be a time of PRAISE. Praise opens the floodgates of the Father's love and mercy. Read quietly or aloud a litany of praise, and allow it to open your spirit and draw you into the realm of the miraculous and into the abundant life in which God created us to live. Add praises of your own! (See Appendix B for the Litany of Praise to Jesus.)

SECOND PRINCIPLE (the Second and Third Petitions): Plan: "Thy Kingdom Come, Thy Will Be Done"

The second life-changing principle is that God the Father has a plan revealed through his Son Jesus in the power of the Spirit for each and every one of His children. This plan He reveals moment by moment and step by step externally through creation, covenant, liturgy and word; and internally, through our own thoughts, deepest intuitions and desires.

Each one of us, like Jesus, can listen to, discern and obey the still voice of the Father within us. Each one of us can allow His rule to reign in our minds, hearts and lives. The secret here is total surrender, that is the entrusting of our minds and hearts to allow God to rule within us as He ruled within Jesus and Mary by the power of His Spirit.

It is the humble realization that all life and all holiness comes from the Father through the Son by the working of the Holy Spirit. It is the faithful recognition that life is a relationship with the source of life, and that is our loving Father. We are here not to live in the kingdom of this world nor in the kingdom of self, but rather in the Kingdom of God. Jesus' main message, especially in the gospel of Matthew, was to live in the Kingdom of God. To allow God to rule our minds with His wisdom and our hearts with His love is to be under the control of His Spirit.

This marvelous Father-God, whom we honor, praise and worship, has a plan for our lives that He reveals step by step and moment by moment, both individually and collectively. God's plan was to send Jesus into the world and into our hearts, enabling us to think, love and act like Jesus. And the power to do that is given to us through the Holy Spirit and His wisdom, heart and power gifts that He pours into us. Therefore, God wants us to ask Him to reveal His Kingdom and His Will.

In James 1:5 it says that if you really want to know what God wants you to do, simply ask Him and He will gladly tell you. We must believe that God speaks or reveals His Plan in such a way that we can hear it and follow it. There are some people who believe that God has only revealed the skeletal outline of that plan through the Bible and the teachings of our Church. There are others who believe that revelation ceased with the death of the last apostle.

But in John 5:19, Jesus stated, "With all the earnestness I possess, I tell you this: the Son does nothing on His own. The Son does only what He sees the Father doing."

Jesus never did His own will. He always listened to, discerned, and obeyed the voice of His Father. His spirituality was to be the Son of the Father. Often He spent the night in prayer in deep communion with God, Yahweh, His Abba. His mission was to do the Father's Will.

We, too, can learn to listen to, discern and obey the Will of the

Father. God speaks all the time, externally through signs, symbols, creations, science, people, Scripture, life experiences, and sacraments. And internally, God speaks to us through our thoughts, insights, and intuitions. He enlightens our mind with His thoughts and inflames our hearts with His desires. He has placed the very Spirit of His Son within us so that we can listen to, discern and obey His voice.

The insight of this prayer is that God speaks to all His children all the time. We can listen to God as He reveals that part of His Kingdom each day and that part of His Will for the moment.

Now is the time to quiet our minds and hearts and spend time listening. I would suggest here *two methods of listening prayer*:

Praying the Scriptures Under the Anointing of the Spirit

In John 5:39, Jesus says to the scribes of His day, "You search the Scriptures thinking that in them you will find life but they reveal Me and you refuse to come to me to find life." He is teaching them and us that the Scriptures, especially the New Testament, must be read with His Spirit opening our eyes to their real meaning. In Luke 24, Jesus talks with His disciples on the road to Emmaus "beginning with Moses and the prophets" and opens their eyes to all the Scriptures taught "concerning Himself." The disciples' response was "were not our hearts burning inside us as He walked with us along the way and opened the Scriptures to us."

This is what Jesus wants to do for each of us — to open the personal, here and now, tailor-made meaning of His Word to us.

We must, therefore, read the Scriptures only under the anointing of His Spirit. To read the Bible with only our eyes will blind us to its real meaning and divide the Church. Behold, today we have well over 26,000 different Protestant denominations, each calling themselves His followers yet each turning from the true Church He founded that day in Caesarea Philippi when He said to Peter, "You are Peter, and upon this rock I will build MY Church" (Mt 16:18).

There is only one Church — so the Scriptures must be read in the context of that Church and her teachings, and under the anointing of His Spirit. If so, they will be understood — "in Christ".

A *Simple Method of Listening Prayer Using Scripture*

Place – Find a quiet place where you can be alone with Christ as you read His Word.

Presence – Put yourself in the presence of Christ by

1) Saying an Act of Consecration to Him — "Lord, I am totally yours. Speak, Your servant is listening."

2) Reciting an Act of Contrition to cleanse your soul of all sin and unforgiveness.

Passage – Ask the Holy Spirit to put into your thoughts a page number or a passage from the Scriptures, preferably the New Testament. "Ask and you will receive." Something will come to you as you ask. Then turn to that page or passage.

Point or Principle – As you read the passage, something will impress you. Some say certain words appear as if "in gold" or something will "hop off the page" or "touch your heart." You will intuitively get the point. It will be personal and practical, such as, "forgive your husband," "go here," "do this," "don't do that," "relax," "forget," "do not worry about that."

Practice – Once you get the personal, practical point or principle, put it into action. Practice it. If Jesus told you to forgive someone, then forgive him. If He told you to do something, do it. "The wise man who built his house upon the rock is he who hears the word of the Lord and obeys it" (Mt 7:24).

Praying by Keeping A Spiritual Journal

Another concrete way of hearing God is to go apart and listen as God speaks to you through your own thoughts, then write them down. It is today called "journaling," but this method has been around for 6,000 years. The first one to keep a journal was Moses. We have five of his journals. We call them the Books of Moses (the first five books of the Bible.) The Bible (literally) itself is a collection of 72 journals. Seventy-two sacred authors wrote down the inspirations of the Holy Spirit. Therefore, we say that God is the primary author and the sacred writer;

Matthew, Luke or John are secondary authors.

A Simple Method of Listening Prayer by Journaling
Six keys to journaling are:

Key One: Quiet yourself. Go off by yourself to a quiet place, sit in a comfortable chair and pray to the Holy Spirit to QUIET your mind of all the "marketplace" thoughts (that is, the worldly, ego-centric, worrying, negative thoughts that tend to fill it).

Key Two: Focus on Jesus. Try to picture Jesus if you are imaginative and intuitive, or think of the word "Jesus" over and over again until your mind is absorbed in Him. When you are absorbed in Him, ask Him to speak to you through your thoughts or intuitions.

Key Three: Be aware of the flow of spontaneous thoughts that come into your mind. They just seem to bubble up from within.

Key Four: Write down in a journal these messages you are receiving in a flow of spontaneous writing, (i.e., these thoughts that are bubbling forth). Have faith that God is answering your prayer. You have asked, now receive in faith.

Key Five: Sort out or discern with Scripture or another spiritual person the messages you are receiving to see if they are from the Holy Spirit, from you or from an evil source. Follow the principles of discernment.

Key Six: Once you are relatively certain (remember, it's a faith journey) that something you received is of God, step out in faith and do it.

THIRD PRINCIPLE (The Fourth Petition): Provision: "Give Us This Day Our Daily Bread"
God wants us to rely upon Him and upon His providential care to supply all of our needs. That is the covenant He has made. Let Me be your God. Let Me provide for everything.

In a materialistic culture where most of us tend to rely more on money than on God, we need to believe that God wants to provide for our daily needs. So use this time of prayer to present your petitions.

Don't buy it, pray for it would be a modern interpretation. It really works. GOD PROVIDES. "ASK AND YOU SHALL RECEIVE."

Those of us in the community at My Father's House Retreat Center have learned to ask. When we were refurbishing our chapel, we needed an altar. So we prayed for one. Shortly afterward, Father George from St. Mary's Ukrainian Church in Colchester, Connecticut gave us a beautiful altar. When we needed a tabernacle, Father Thomas Goekler from Sacred Heart in Hartford called and gave us a tabernacle. We needed pews. Monsignor Normand Methe from St. Mary's in Stamford gave us the pews. On and on it went. God provides. He's more reliable, practical and economical than money. Besides, as Jesus tells us, you can't put your faith in God AND money; it's one or the other.

One fourth of the teachings of Jesus teach us to rely more on the Father and less on money. He must have seen how difficult it would be for a materialistic people to get the point. *Don't rely on money, rely on My Father to give you your daily food, bread, shoes, transportation, rent, clothing, and so forth.* Look at the birds. It works. Look at the flowers. It works. Look at Him. It works.

> "Therefore I tell you, do not worry about your life, what you will eat or drink; or about your body, what you will wear. Is not life more important than food, and the body more important than clothes? Look at the birds of the air; they do not sow or reap or store away in barns, and yet your heavenly Father feeds them. Are you not much more valuable than they? Who of you by worrying can add a single hour to his life? And why do you worry about clothes? See how the lilies of the field grow. They do not labor or spin" (Mt 6:25-28).

As these verses from Matthew tell us, nothing is more important in our spiritual life than to say *Yes* to Jesus with all our heart and soul, and then to let the Holy Spirit work out its meaning in our life. God loves us without measure and will always be with us, protecting us and guiding us. The more we open up, yield and simply allow ourselves to be drawn deeply into the Lord's love, the more our lives will be directed and come into alignment with God's Will.

Recite the following prayer daily and notice the changes it makes in your life as you begin to turn everything over to the Lord and trust in His tender mercy.

A PRAYER OF SURRENDER
"...may Your will be done" (Mt 26:42)

Loving Father,

I surrender to You today with all my heart and soul. Please come into my heart in a deeper way. I say "Yes," to You today. I open all the secret places of my heart to You and say, "Come on in." Jesus, You are Lord of my whole life. I believe in You and receive You as my Lord and Savior. I hold nothing back.

Holy Spirit, bring me to a deeper conversion to the person of Jesus Christ. I surrender all to You: my time, my treasure, my talent, my health, my family, my resources, my work, relationships, time management, successes and failures. I release them and let them go.

I surrender my understanding of how things ought to be, my choices and my will. I surrender to You the promises I have kept and the promises I have failed to keep. I surrender my weaknesses and strengths to You. I surrender my emotions, my fears, my insecurities, my sexuality. I especially surrender (here mention other areas of surrender as the Holy Spirit reveals them to you.)

Lord, I surrender my entire life to You - the past, the present and the future. In sickness and in health, in life and in death, I belong to You. (Remain with the Lord in a spirit of silence through your thoughts, a heart song or simply staying in His presence and listening for His voice.)

Here is another prayer of surrender penned by St. Ignatius that has been passed down through the ages.

> Take, Lord, and receive, all my liberty,
> my memory, my understanding,
> and my whole will.
> You have given me all that I have,
> all that I am,
> and I surrender all to Your Divine will.
> Give me only Your love and Your grace.
> With this I am rich enough,
> and I have no more to ask.
>
> Amen.

We will find that as we surrender everything, we receive everything, as this reflection indicates.

> I asked God for strength, that I might achieve,
> I was made weak, that I might learn humbly to obey.
> I asked for health, that I might do greater things,
> I was given infirmity, that I might do better things.
> I asked for riches, that I might be happy,
> I was given poverty, that I might be wise.
> I asked for power, that I might have the praise of men,
> I was given weakness, that I might feel the need of God.
> I asked for all things, that I might enjoy life,
> I was given life, that I might enjoy all things.
> I got nothing that I asked for, but everything I had hoped for.
> Almost despite myself, my unspoken prayers were answered.
> I am among all mankind, most richly blessed!

As we become poor in spirit, we receive greater blessings than ever — worshipers in spirit and in truth.

FOURTH PRINCIPLE (the Fifth Petition): Personal Forgiveness: "Forgive Us Our Trespasses As We Forgive Those Who Trespass Against Us"

This principle is explosive. Let God forgive you and you forgive others. FORGIVENESS IS GOD'S ANSWER. It flows from His love and mercy, His "hesed" (*Heb*: mercy) and "emeth" (*Heb*: love). It's the only real answer.

Even today after the coming of Jesus, most men and women live lives burdened with guilt and with shame. Psychologists have no answer for this. What they do tell us, however, is that most people handle guilt, bitterness, hatred or shame using one or more of four mechanisms: repression, denial, rationalization, and projection. But it doesn't go away.

Jesus, after His horrendous death and glorious resurrection to save us from sin and shame, appeared to the apostles on Easter Sunday evening through closed doors. He said to them, "As the Father has sent Me, so do I send you." Then he breathed on them and said, "Receive the Holy Spirit. Whose sins you shall forgive they are forgiven, and whose sins you shall retain, they are held bound" (Jn 20:22-23).

As Catholic Christians, we have the only practical, powerful, fool-proof answer to guilt, bitterness, hatred and shame. It is FORGIVENESS through confession. Because God holds us responsible for every one of our thoughts, words, actions, attitudes and motives, He — in the abundance and richness of His mercy — has given to us in the Sacrament of Reconciliation a way out of these negative emotions.

We used to call it penance, but it really is a sacrament of love, a sacrament that lets us allow Jesus to take away everything that divides and destroys us from living in the presence and loving union with God.

The Sacrament of Reconciliation

There are six steps we can take to make a meaningful confession:

Step One: *Examine your conscience* – Don't be hasty. Don't be superficial. Avoid anxiety and prepare to tell your sins to the priest honestly, simply and with sincere contrition.

Many sins are mortal and the Eucharist is forbidden until a good confession is made to a priest. If in doubt whether a sin is mortal or venial, confess it and consult a good catechism or priest who is very loyal to the Holy Father and to Rome's teachings. A *mortal sin* involves a serious matter. It occurs when sufficient reflection takes place and is committed with full consent of the will. A *venial sin* refers to less serious acts and attitudes which fail to help us grow in our loving relationship with God or weaken the relationship.

1. Have I denied or doubted God's existence? Have I refused to believe God's revelation? How often have I broken the First Commandment by giving more of my heart to my job, my family, my pleasure, my interests, my finances? How often have I truly worshipped God? How often have I put Him first in my life? Have I doubted or presumed upon God's mercy? Have I neglected prayer for a long time? Have I denied that I am a Catholic? Did I leave the Catholic faith? Have I been involved with New Age or the occult -- ouija boards, horoscopes, tarot cards, fortune tellers, seances, spiritism, Silva Mind Control, EST, Transcendental Meditation, Eastern Religions, etc.?

2. Have I taken the Lord's name in vain or blasphemed God or sworn? Have I broken an oath or vow?

3. Have I missed Mass on Sunday or performed unnecessary work on Sunday? Did I really make it the "Lord's Day"? Am I always reverent in the presence of Jesus in the most Blessed Sacrament? Was I inattentive at Mass? Did I come to Mass late or leave Mass early?

4. Have I obeyed all lawful authority (parents, boss, police, government, etc.)? Have I neglected my duties to my husband, wife, children, or parents? Have I failed to actively take an interest in the religious education and formation of my children? Have I failed to educate myself on the true teachings of the Church? Have I given a full day's work in return for my full day's pay? Have I given a fair wage to my employee?

5. Did I agree that killing is allowable? Am I "Pro-Choice" on the abortion questions? Have I had or consented to an abortion or assisted another in obtaining one? Have I consented to murder in any of its forms? Have I contributed to destructive gossip? Was I impatient, angry, envious, unkind, proud, jealous, revengeful, hateful toward others, or

lazy? Did I set a bad example, abuse drugs, drink alcohol to excess, fight or quarrel?

6. Have I been impure in thought, word or action either alone or with another (including promiscuity, homosexuality, adultery, fornication, immoral books, videos, conversations, innuendoes, or jokes)? Have I committed adultery against God through spiritual infidelity? Have I caused a scandal by what I said or did, especially to the young? Was I the cause of anyone leaving the faith?

7. Have I stolen?

8. Have I lied?

9. Have I desired another's spouse?

10. Have I been content with my own goods? Have I been envious of another? Have I been proud — looking down at others because of race, appearance, ethnic origin, manner of dress, economic level, etc.?

Precepts of the Church
Have I also attended Mass on Holy Days?
Do I go to confession often?
Do I receive communion often?
Do I respect the laws of the Church concerning marriage?
Do I contribute my time, talent and treasure to my parish?

Step Two: Be truly sorry for your sins and make a firm purpose not to sin again.

Step Three: Forgive everyone who has ever hurt you or harmed you in any way.

Step Four: Go to confession (i.e., confess your sins to a priest in the beautiful healing Sacrament of Reconciliation, as shown below).

Procedure in the Confessional

The priest may begin with a Scripture reading. After he finishes, you say: "Bless me, Father, in this confession. It has been — (state length of time, i.e., number of weeks or months) — since my last confession.

I accuse myself of the following sins."

Then tell your mortal sins and the number of times committed. If you have no mortal sins to confess, then confess two or three venial sins you have committed since your last confession. When you have finished telling your sins, you should say: *"For these and all the sins of my past life, especially for my sins of — I am truly sorry."*

The priest now gives the necessary advice, assigns your penance and asks you to say the *Act of Contrition.* Then wait and listen as the priest gives the absolution. Then say *Thank You, Father,* and leave the confessional and perform the penance assigned by the priest.

Act of Contrition
O my God, I am heartily sorry for having offended Thee, and I detest all my sins, because I dread the loss of heaven and the pains of hell. But most of all because they have offended Thee, my God, Who art all good and deserving of all my love. I firmly resolve, with the help of Thy grace, to confess my sins, do penance and to amend my life. Amen.

Step Five: Thank God for His love and mercy (for dying on the Cross so that you could be set free from guilt by the Blood of Jesus).

Step Six: Do the penance the priest gave you.

The only answer is God's answer – FORGIVENESS. And the only thing that God asks us is to PASS IT ON. FORGIVE OTHERS AS I FORGIVE YOU. So now that we've asked to be forgiven, we need to forgive those against whom we carry buried emotions of anger, bitterness and resentment. Decide to be reconciled with all the people in your life. Set them free and set yourself free in the process. Break the chains of unforgiveness and let go of anything that you hold against another person.

Offer the following prayer of forgiveness for 30 days, and release the burdens that you hold deep in your heart.

Forgiveness Prayer
Loving Father,

I choose to forgive everyone in my life, including myself, because You have forgiven me. Thank You, Lord, for this grace. I forgive myself for all my sins, faults and failings, especially for (*mention specific failings*). I forgive myself for not being perfect. I accept myself and make a decision to stop picking on myself and being my own worst enemy. I release the things held against myself, free myself from bondage and make peace with myself today, by the power of the Holy Spirit.

I forgive my MOTHER for any negativity and unlove she may have extended to me throughout my life, knowingly or unknowingly, especially for (*mention a specific event or negative behavior*). For any abuse of any sort, I do forgive her today. For any way that she did not provide a deep, full, satisfying mother's blessing, I do forgive her today. I release her from bondage and make peace with her today.

I forgive my FATHER for any negativity and unlove he may have extended to me throughout my life, knowingly or unknowingly, especially for (*mention a specific event or negative behavior*). For any and all abuses, unkind acts, hurts, and deprivations, I do forgive him today. For any way that I did not receive a full, satisfying father's blessing, I forgive him today. I release him from bondage and make peace with him today.

I forgive my SPOUSE for any negativity and unlove extended throughout our time together, especially for (*mention a specific event or negative behavior*). For all the wounds of our relationship, I do forgive my spouse today. I release my spouse from bondage and make peace between us today.

I forgive my CHILDREN for any hurts, especially for (*mention a specific time or behavior*). I release them from bondage and make peace with them today. Bless them, Lord.

I forgive my SISTERS and BROTHERS for any negativity and unlove, especially for (mention a specific event or negative behavior). I forgive my BLOOD RELATIVES for any abuses, especially for (*mention abuses*). I forgive my ANCESTORS for any negative actions that affect my life today and make it harder for me today to live in the freedom of a child of God. I release them from bondage and make peace with them today, in Jesus' name.

I forgive my FRIENDS for any actions of negativity and unlove, especially for (*mention a specific event or negative action*). For any time they abused our relationship or led me astray, I do forgive them. I release them from all bondage and make peace with them today, in the power of the Holy Spirit.

I forgive my EMPLOYERS of the present and the past for any negativity and unlove, especially for (*be specific*). I release them from all bondage and pray a blessing on them today, in Jesus' name.

I forgive all SCHOOL TEACHERS for any negative, abusive actions, especially for (*be specific*).

I forgive all LAWYERS, DOCTORS, NURSES, and other professionals, especially for (*be specific*).

I forgive CLERGY and all representatives of the Church, especially for (*mention*). I release them all, in Jesus' name.

I forgive every member of SOCIETY who has hurt me in any way; those who have hurt me by criminal action or who have harmed my family. I forgive all in public life who have passed laws opposing Christian values. I forgive all the unfair, anonymous sources of pain and annoyance in my life.

Heavenly Father, I now ask for the grace to forgive the ONE PERSON IN LIFE WHO HAS HURT ME THE MOST. The one who is the hardest to forgive, I now choose to forgive, though I may still feel angry and hurt. I also make peace with the one family member, the one friend and the one authority figure who has hurt me the most.

Lord, is there anyone else I need to forgive? (Be still and listen.)

Thank You, loving Father, for setting me free.

I now pray a blessing on those who have hurt me. Lord, do something special for each of them today. Thank You, Lord. I praise You! Amen.

FIFTH PRINCIPLE (The Sixth And Seventh Petitions): Power/Protection "Lead Us Not Into Temptation, But Deliver Us From Evil"

God is our Protector. He really is. He warns us of all impending evil: spiritually from sin, emotionally from worldly depression and fear, and physically from any danger. We have to learn how to hear His voice so that we will heed His warnings.

God does not tempt us. He allows temptation but temptation comes from the world of flesh and from the devil — not from God.

In the first chapter of the epistle of St. James, James states this so explicitly. God leads us through temptation to victory. God is with us in the fiery heat of temptation to guide us and to deliver us. Not only does God tell us where to go, but also where not to go. Not only does God tell us what to do, but what not to do. He tells us to think loving, pure, kind, and generous thoughts, realizing that the meditations of our minds will become the desires of our hearts.

Jesus spends much time teaching about mental attitudes. The more our mindset is to be loving, poor, generous, humble and obedient, the more our desires and actions will follow suit. *Wisdom in the mind leads to love in the heart and holiness in the action.* Once our minds and hearts are renewed, our lives and actions will resist evil.

In the sixth chapter of St. Paul's epistle to the Ephesians, Paul tells us how to put on the armor of God (see Appendix B). In his *first principle*, he tells us to put on salvation as a helmet. He uses here the imagery of the Roman soldier fully equipped for battle. The helmet of salvation as a mindset is simply the realization that God is with us, that He loves us, and that He will provide for a way out of the temptation or trial.

Next in the *second principle*, He tells us to put on the breastplate of righteousness, that is to confess all unknown sin so that Satan is not given any toehold within us. Frequent confession is a tremendous remedy against temptation. Then Paul tells us to put on the belt of truth, that is to live in the light. By living truthfully and honestly, we deny the forces of darkness that enter into our attitudes.

Those who live in darkness sooner or later will act in darkness. Those who live in the light will act in the light. An honest and truthful person becomes a transparent person. People immediately see their sincerity, humility and goodness.

The *third principle* is to take up the sword and the Spirit which is the Word of God. The more we meditate and put into action the principles of God's Word, especially the Gospel of Jesus, the stronger we will be against any temptation.

The *fourth principle* is to take up faith as a shield. As the young men in the fiery furnace in Daniel had faith that God would protect them in the midst of the fire, so our faith becomes a protective shield against the fiery darts of the adversary who puts evil thoughts in our minds, if not to tempt us, at least to harass us.

And the *fifth principle* of the armor is to put on the shoes of spreading the gospel. The more we try to influence others to be holy, the holier we will become. The more we say to another, that dishonesty, lack of charity and worldliness are wrong, the more we will believe and live them myself.

God does not want us to crash into the obstacles in the minefield of life. He warns us of their coming and shows us a way out. The following is a prayer for protection that God will always keep us in His care as our loving, devoted Father.

PRAYER OF PROTECTION

Dear Heavenly Father, You are our Protector. You shield us from temptation and evil as we rely upon Your guidance and listen to Your Spirit. You lead us not with temptation, but warn us of all impending evil — spiritual, emotional and physical. Help us to stay attuned to Your still voice from within that tells us to be alert to the dangers that surround us. You deliver us from all evil as Your Spirit guides us step by step into the safety of Your Kingdom. Send Your angels to protect me and my loved ones from all harm. Deliver us from all evil in the name of Your Son, Jesus, I pray. Amen.

Becoming Still in Silence Before God
"Be still and know that I am God" (Ps 46:10).

A beautiful image of prayer is found in the magnificent story of Elijah who heard God not in the thunder but in the still voice of the breeze.

We live on two consciousness levels. On the surface, at the level of the ego and marketplace, all sorts of hurried, frantic and distracting thoughts compete for attention. But deep within the Spirit of God is prayer. If we learn to go beneath the outer self and center ourselves, we can literally flow with the Spirit.

In all methods of prayer, God must teach us how to be still. Here is Mother Teresa of Calcutta's powerful meditation on silence:

"If we really want to pray, we must first learn to listen, for in the silence of the heart, God speaks. And to be able to experience that silence, to be able to hear God, we need a clean heart, for a clean heart can see God, can hear God, can listen to God.

When it is difficult to pray, we must help ourselves to do so. The first means is through silence, for souls of prayer are souls of great silence. We cannot put ourselves directly in the presence of God if we do not practice internal and external silence.

God is the friend of silence.

Let us adore Jesus in our hearts, who spent thirty years out of thirty-three in silence, who began His public life by spending forty days in silence, who often retired alone to spend the night on a mountain in silence. He who spoke with authority, now spends His earthly life in silence. Let us adore Jesus in the eucharistic silence.

We need to find God and He cannot be found in noise and restlessness. See how nature, the trees, the flowers, the grass grow in perfect silence – see the stars, the moon and the sun, how they move in silence. Is not our mission to give God to the poor in the slums? Not a dead God but a living, loving God. The more we receive in silent prayer, the more we can give in our active life.

Silence gives us a new outlook on everything. We need silence to be able to touch souls. The essential thing is not what we say but what God says to us and through us. Jesus is always waiting for us in silence. In that silence He will listen to us, there He will speak to our soul, and there we will hear His voice. Interior silence is very difficult, but we must make the effort.

In silence, we will find new energy and true unity. The energy of God will be ours to do all things well. The unity of our thoughts with His thoughts, the unity of our prayers with His prayers, the unity of our actions with His actions, of our life with His life. All our words will be useless, unless they come from within – words which do not give the light of Christ increase the darkness."

Deep prayer and contemplation are a response to the love of God. It does not start with active efforts or anxious striving on our part, but with love powerfully experienced. St. John is quite clear on this point: "In this is love, not that we loved God, but that He loved us." In the silence of our hearts, this love is like a call which is invariably creative – evoking a response, an interior movement of the soul towards God, energy. This is the energy which enables Mother Teresa and others like her to fuse a life of prayer with a life of action. The one is totally dependent on the other. Her tremendous achievements depend for their efficacy on a receptive, listening silence. Here's another prayer that makes the point.

> Lord, teach us that even as the wonder of the stars in heaven only reveals itself in the silence of the night, so the wonder of God reveals itself in the silence of the soul. That in the silence of our hearts we may see the scattered leaves of all the universe bound by love.
> ~ Adapted from the Bhagavad Gita

Steps to Becoming Still
In order to become still, there are certain steps that we can take:

Remove outer noise
1. Get away from television, the telephone and other business around you. Go off by yourself to a quiet place.

2. Remove all physical tension by sitting in a comfortable location.

3. Tap into the quietness of the world in the early morning

or late evening.

Remove inner noise:

1. Still thoughts of things to do by writing them down in a spontaneous flow and setting them aside for later.

2. Still thoughts of sin. Confess your sins to Jesus and receive His forgiveness. Resolve to go to confession if necessary. Be bathed in the blood of His forgiveness.

3. Still fluttering thoughts by focusing on Jesus. Say His name "Jesus" over and again, keeping time with your breathing.

4. Try to get in touch with your heart. Begin singing softly and listening to the spontaneous song bubbling up from your heart.

It is important to write your thoughts so that you can discern or sort them out at a later time with Scripture, a spiritual director or friend in the Lord. Our memory is not as good a day, a week or a month later. So you need to literally get these ideas down in black and white so you can look at them, reflect upon what you've written and see how your thoughts change and evolve over time.

Driving the car or waiting at a red light is a wonderful time for quiet prayer. Some thoughts will begin to bubble forth, such as: "My beloved child, listen carefully; all is well. Look only to Me. Listen to Me. I will guide you gently and at all times. Stop. Look. Listen. Stop your frantic activity. Look unto Me. Listen to My Words."

You will soon be able to sense inner stillness as:

1. Not doing anything. There is no striving or trying hard; just relaxing and surrendering — in other words, letting go.

2. Being in touch with the Lord.

3. Experiencing His presence in the NOW, in the moment; knowing Him as the great I AM.

4. Sharing this moment with His in love, praise and worship

using your 'inner eyes'.

5. Something that is not forced or hurried.

6. Something that just happens.

7. Experiencing an attitude of relaxed living.

8. Simply abiding, as a branch to a vine.

Examples of virtues that are required:

Humility – Be willing to be alone with the Alone, of being a child with His Abba.

Contrition – Repent of any known sin.

Fruit – Really believe that God is within us and wants to make His presence felt.

Patience – Give Him all the time He wants.

Trust – Trust Him to respond.

On Earth As It Is In Heaven

What would happen if everyone prayed and lived the *Our Father* as Jesus taught? What would happen if everyone throughout the day would spend their time praising God, seeking and following His Plan and Will, depending upon Him for everything that they needed, that is — just living out of the Covenant where God would be God and we would be His people, receiving and giving His Love and Forgiveness, and allowing Him to protect us from all danger and sin? The answer is in the *Our Father*, itself. Then the Kingdom of God would come on earth as it is in heaven.

This is God's Plan, that heaven would be on earth. Meditate upon the full significance of the Father's Plan, not only to make us sons and daughters of God, but to bring more and more of the protection, beauty, order and love of heaven to earth. For in heaven, there is no sickness. God's ultimate desire is that there be no sickness on earth. In heaven there is no sin. God's ultimate plan is for a sinless world. In heaven, no one dies. The deepest desire of God's Heart is to bring everyone eternal life.

Summary

In the *Our Father*, Jesus has taught us the principles of the Kingdom of God so that heaven on earth becomes a reality. As we seek to praise Him, to seek His Plan, to live by His Provisions, and to be gifted with His Mercy and Protection, the Covenant that He made through Adam, Noah, Abraham, Moses, Ezrah, David, and ultimately with Jesus will come not only to its fulfillment but to its fruition and perfection, as well; so that we, "with unveiled faces, will reflect like mirrors the brightness of the Son of God who is our glory. For it is the work of the Spirit to transform us from glory into glory into Jesus, whom we reflect" (2 Cor. 3:18).

CHAPTER II

THE LORD'S PRAYER
by Saint Thomas Aquinas

aint Thomas Aquinas preached a series of fifty-nine sermons during Lent in 1273, the last year of his life, that were devoted to simple Christian faith and prayers. It is likely that ten sermons were devoted to the Lord's Prayer alone. The sermons are remarkable for their clarity, their depth, their holiness, and their wealth of Scriptural quotations. What follows here is Thomas's commentary on The *Lord's Prayer* and why he considers it to be the most perfect prayer.

I. PRAYER

Among all prayers, the Lord's Prayer[1] stands preeminent, for it excels in the five conditions required in prayer: confidence, rectitude, order, devotion, and humility.

A. Conditions required for prayer.

1. Confidence. Prayer should be confident: "Let us go with confidence to the throne of grace"[2] (and with fullness of faith: "Let him ask in faith nothing wavering").[3] There can be no doubt that the Lord's Prayer affords the greatest security, since it was framed by our Advocate and most wise Petitioner, in Whom are "all the treasures of wisdom"[4] and of Whom it is said: "We have an advocate with the Father, Jesus Christ, the just."[5] Hence, Cyprian says: "Seeing that we have Christ as an advocate with the Father for our sins, we should employ the words of our Advocate when we seek forgiveness of our sins."[6]

The trustworthiness of this prayer is even more apparent because He Who (with the Father) hears our prayer, Himself taught us how to pray, according to Psalm 90:15: "He shall cry to me and I will hear him." For that reason, Cyprian says that "to plead with our Lord in His own words betokens the prayer of an intimate and devoted friend."[7] Consequently, this prayer is never fruitless, seeing that according to Augustine venial sins are forgiven by means of it.[8]

2. Rectitude. Prayer should have rectitude, so that we ask God for that which is good for us. For Damascene says that "to pray is to ask fitting things of God."[9] It often happens that our prayers are not granted because we ask for that which is not good for us: "You ask and receive not, because you ask amiss."[10]

Now, it is no easy matter to know what we should pray for, since it is difficult to know what we ought to desire. For if it is right to pray for a certain thing, it must be right to desire it. For this reason, the Apostle says that "we know not what we should pray for as we ought."[11]

Now, Christ is our teacher; it belongs to Him to teach us what we ought to pray for. Thus, His disciples said to Him, "Lord, teach us to pray."[12] It follows, then, that we pray most rightly when we ask for what He taught us to pray for. Hence, Augustine says, "If we would pray rightly and fittingly, we should say nothing else but what is contained in this prayer of our Lord."[13]

3. Order. As desire should be orderly, so should prayer, since it is the expression of desire. Now the right order is that our desires and prayers should prefer spiritual goods to carnal goods and heavenly things to earthly things: "Seek ye first the kingdom of God and His justice, and all these things shall be added unto you."[14] Our Lord teaches us to observe this order in the Lord's Prayer, in which we pray first for heavenly and afterwards for earthly blessings.

4. Devoutness. Prayer should be devout, because the unction of devotion makes the sacrifice of prayer acceptable to God: "In Thy name I will lift up my hands; let my soul be filled as with marrow and fatness."[15] Yet it often happens that devotion grows cool through prayer being too long. For that reason, our Lord warned us against praying at unnecessary length: "When you are praying, speak not much."[16] And Augustine says to Proba: "Beware of praying with many words: it is fervent attention that secures a hearing."[17] Hence, the brevity of the Lord's Prayer.

Now, devotion arises from charity, which is the love of God and of our neighbor, and both of these are indicated in the Lord's Prayer. In order to express our love of God, we call Him *Father*, and in order to indicate love of our neighbor, we pray for all in general: *Our Father…*

Forgive us our trespasses (since it is through love of our neighbor that we make this petition).

5. Humility. Prayer should be humble: "He hath had regard to the prayer of the humble."[18] This is seen in the story of the Pharisee and the publican, [19] and is expressed in the words of Judith: "The prayer of the humble and the meek hath always pleased Thee."[20] This same humility is observed in the Lord's Prayer since true humility consists in not presuming on our own strength, but in trusting to obtain all things from the power of God.

B. Benefits of prayer
Prayer brings about three benefits:

1. It remedies evils. Prayer is an efficacious and useful remedy against all kinds of evils. Hence, it delivers a man from sins already committed: "Thou hast forgiven the wickedness of my sin; for this shall every godly man pray to Thee."[21] Thus, the thief on his cross prayed and obtained pardon: "This day shalt thou be with me in paradise."[22] So also the publican prayed and "went down to his house justified."[23]

Prayer also frees man from the fear of future sin and from trials and despondency: "Is any one of you in trouble? Let him pray."[24] Again, it delivers him from persecutors and enemies: "Instead of making me a return for my love, they decried me; but I gave myself to prayer."[25]

2. It obtains that which we desire. Prayer is efficacious and useful for obtaining whatever we desire: "All things whatsoever ye ask, when ye pray, believe that you shall receive."[26] And if our prayer is not granted, it is either because it lacks constancy, in that "we should pray always and never faint"[27] or because we ask for what is less conducive to our salvation. Thus, Augustine says, "Of His bounty, the Lord often grants not what we seek, so as to bestow something preferable." We have an example of this in Paul who three times prayed for the removal of the thorn in his flesh, and yet was not heard.[28]

3. It establishes friendship with God. Prayer is profitable because it makes us the familiars of God: "let my prayer be directed as incense in Thy sight."[29]

II. OUR FATHER

Accordingly He begins, *Our Father*. We must consider two things here: 1) in what sense God is our Father, and 2) what we owe Him because He is our Father.

A. Why we call God *Father*

1. He created us. We call God *Father* because He created us in a special way — namely, in His own image and likeness which He did not impress on other creatures here below: "He is thy Father Who made thee, and created thee."[30]

2. He governs us. We also call God *Father* because He governs us. For although He governs *all* things, yet He governs us as masters of ourselves whereas He governs other things as slaves of His will: "Thy providence, O Father, governs all things."[31] "Thou disposest of us with great favor."[32]

3. He adopted us. We call God *Father* because He has adopted us. For He endowed other creatures with trifling gifts, but to us He granted the inheritance, because (as the Apostle says) we are His sons "and if sons, heirs also."[33] "You have not received the spirit of bondage again in fear, but you have received the spirit of adoption of sons whereby we cry, Abba ('Father')."[34]

B. What we owe God as our Father
Our debt to God is fourfold:

1. Honor. We owe God honor: "If I am Father, where is my honor?"[35] This honor consists in three things:

    a. In reference to Himself, we should honor God by giving Him praise: "The sacrifice of praise shall honor me."[36] Moreover, this praise should be not only on our lips, but also in our heart: "This people honoreth me with their lips, but their heart is far from me."[37]

    b. In reference to ourselves, we should honor God by purity of body: "Glorify and bear God in your body."[38]

    c. In reference to our neighbor, we should honor God by

judging Him justly: "The king's honor loveth judgment."[39]

2. Imitation. We owe God imitation, since He is our Father: "Thou shalt call me Father and shalt not cease to walk after Me."[40] This is done in three ways:

a. By loving Him. We imitate God by loving Him: "Be ye imitators of God as most dear children and walk in love."[41] And this must be in the heart.

b. By showing mercy. We imitate God by being merciful, because mercy is bound to accompany love: "Be ye merciful."[42] And this must be in deed.

c. By being perfect. We imitate God by being perfect, since love and mercy should be perfect: "Be ye perfect as also your heavenly Father is perfect."[43]

3. Obedience. We owe God obedience: "Shall we not much more obey the Father of spirits?"[44] We owe Him obedience.

a. Because of His dominion, for He is the Lord: "All that the Lord hath said will we do, and be obedient."[45]

b. Because of His example, since His true Son was made obedient to the Father unto death.[46]

c. Because obedience is good for us: "I will pray before the Lord Who hath chosen me."[47]

4. Patience. We owe God patience under His chastening: "My son, reject not the correction of the Lord and do not faint when thou art chastised by Him: for whom the Lord loveth, He chastiseth even as a father the son in whom he delighteth."[48]

C. What we owe our neighbor (*our* Father)

From this we are given to understand that we owe our neighbor two things:

1. Love. We owe our neighbor love, because he is our brother, seeing that we are God's children: "He that loveth not his brother whom he seeth, how can he love God Whom he seeth not?"[49]

2. Reverence. We owe our neighbor reverence, because he is a child of God: "Have we not all one father? Hath not one God created us? Why then doth every one of us despise his brother?"[50] "With honor preventing one another."[51]

We do this for the sake of its fruits, since God Himself "became to all that obey Him the cause of eternal salvation."[52]

III. WHO ART IN HEAVEN
A. Confidence in prayer
Of all the things required of us when we pray, confidence is of great avail: "Let him ask in faith, nothing wavering."[53] For this reason, our Lord, in teaching us how to pray, mentions those things which instill confidence in us, such as the loving kindness of a father implied in the words, *Our Father*. Thus, He says, "If ye being evil know how to give good gifts to your children, how much more shall your heavenly Father give the good Spirit to them that ask Him?"[54]

B. Meaning of *Who art in heaven*
Such also is the greatness of His power that He says, *Who art in heaven*. Thus it is written: "Unto Thee have I lifted up mine eyes, Who dwelleth in the heavens."[55]

The phrase, *Who art in heaven*, may be taken to refer to three things:

1. The glory of heaven (which prepares him who prays).
Who art in heaven prepares the man who prays: "Before prayer prepare thy soul."[56] In this way, *in heaven* signifies the glory of heaven: "Your reward is very great in heaven."[57]

We should prepare for prayer:

a. By imitating heavenly things, for a son should imitate his father: "As we have borne the image of the earthly, let us bear the image of the heavenly."[58]

b. By contemplating heavenly things, for a man is wont to turn his thoughts more often toward where his father is, and where those things are that he loves: "Wheresoever thy treasure is, there also is thy heart."[59] "Our conversation is in heaven."[60]

c. By searching for heavenly things, so that from Him Who is in heaven we seek nothing but what is heavenly: "Seek the things that are above where Christ is."[61]

2. The nearness of the Hearer (in the saints). Who are in *heaven* may be taken to indicate the handiness of the Hearer, insofar as God is near to us. Thus, *in caelis* (literally, "in the heavens") would mean "in the saints" in whom God dwells: "Thou, O Lord, art among us."[62] For the saints are called *the heavens* according to the Psalm: "The heavens declare the glory of God."[63]

Now God dwells in the saints in three ways:

a. By faith: "That Christ may dwell in your hearts by faith."[64]

b. By love: "He that dwelleth in love, dwelleth in God, and God in him"[65]; and

c. By the fulfillment of His commandments: "If any man love me, he will keep my word and my Father will love him, and we will come unto him, and make our abode with him."[66]

3. The power of the Hearer. *Who art in heaven* may be taken as referring to the power of the Hearer, so that *the heavens* would signify the heavenly bodies. Not that God is confined within corporeal heavens (for "The heaven and heaven of heavens cannot contain Thee"[67]) but rather that:

a. God is all-seeing in His survey of things because He views them from on high: "He hath looked down from the height of His sanctuary"[68]; and that,

b. He surpasses all things in His might: "The Lord hath prepared His throne in heaven"[69]; and that,

c. He dwells in an unchangeable eternity: "Thou endurest forever"[70] and "Thy years shall not fail."[71] Hence, it is said of Christ: "I will make His throne as the days of heaven."[72] Thus, the Philosopher[73] says that on account of the heavens being incorruptible, all are agreed that heaven is the abode of spirits.[74]

C. These words give us confidence in prayer

Accordingly [as will be shown], the words *Who art in heaven* inspire us with confidence in praying, because of: 1) the power of Him to Whom we pray; 2) our familiar relations with Him; and 3) the nature of our petitions.

1. Because of the power of Him to Whom we pray, which is implied if by *heaven* we understand the corporeal heavens. Although God is not confined within corporeal space (since it is said: "I fill heaven and earth"[75]) yet He is said to be in the corporeal heavens in order to indicate two things: a) the extent of His power, and b) the sublimity of His nature:

> **a. The extent of His power** is maintained against those who assert that all happenings are the necessary result of fate as dependent on the heavenly bodies (accordingly to which opinion it would be useless to seek to obtain anything by praying to God). But this is foolish because God is said to be in heaven in the sense that He is the Lord of the heavens and of the stars: "The Lord hath prepared His throne in the heavens."[76]

> **b. The sublimity of His nature** is maintained against those who in praying suppose and fancy God to exist under certain corporeal images. Thus God is said to be "in heaven" to indicate His supereminence by means of that which is highest among sensible things. For He surpasses all things (including man's desire and understanding). Hence, it is impossible to think or desire anything but what is less than God. Thus, it is said: "Behold, God is great, exceeding our knowledge"[77] and "The Lord is high above all nations"[78] and "To whom have ye likened God?"[79]

2. Because of our familiar relations with God, which are indicated if we take the *heavens* to signify the saints. For on account of His exalted nature, some have asserted that He did not care for human affairs, citing Job: "He walketh about the poles of heaven, and He doth not consider our things."[80] Thus, we need to bear in mind that He is near to us, nay, within us, since He is said to be in the heavens, i.e., in the saints who are called *the heavens*: "The heavens declare the glory of God"[81] and "Thou, O Lord, art among us."[82]

Now, for two reasons, this brings confidence to those who pray:

a. God's nearness. Confidence comes from God's nearness: "The Lord is nigh unto all that call upon Him."[83] Hence, it is said, "But thou when thou prayest enter into thy chamber,"[84] i.e., into your heart.

b. The patronage of the saints. Confidence comes from our ability (by the patronage of the saints) to obtain what we ask for: "Turn to some of the saints."[85] "Pray for one another that ye may be saved."[86]

3. Because of the eternal goods for which we pray. The usefulness and fittingness of prayer are indicated by the words *in heaven*, if by *heaven* is understood spiritual and eternal goods in which beatitude consists, and this is for two reasons:

a. This awakens heavenly desire. Thereby, the words *in heaven* increase our desire for heavenly things since our desire must tend toward where our Father dwells, because there is our inheritance: "Seek the things that are above."[87] "Unto an inheritance incorruptible... reserved in heaven for you."[88]

b. This gives heavenly life. Prayer gives life a spiritual form and conforms us to our heavenly Father: "Such as is the heavenly, such also are they that are heavenly."[89] These two (heavenly desire and heavenly life) equip a man for prayer and enable him to pray in a fitting manner.

IV. HALLOWED BE THY NAME (First Petition)

In this first petition, we ask that God's name be manifested and heralded in us.

A. Characteristics of God's name.

1. God's name is wonderful, because in all creatures it works wonders.

Thus, our Lord said, "In my name they shall cast out devils; they shall speak strange tongues; they shall take up serpents; and if they drink any deadly thing it shall not hurt them."[90]

2. God's name is lovable: "There is no other name under heaven given among men whereby we must be saved"[91] and we should all desire to be saved. We have an example in St. Ignatius, to whom Christ's name was so dear that when Trajan ordered him to deny it, he answered that it could not be dragged from his mouth. And when the emperor threatened to behead him so as to take Christ's name out of his mouth, he replied, "Even though you take it from my mouth, you will never take it from my heart; for it is imprinted on my heart, and therefore, I cannot cease to invoke it." Hearing this and wishing to put it to the test, Trajan, after the servant of God had been beheaded, commanded his heart to be taken out, where it was found to be inscribed with Christ's name in "letters of gold" for he had engraved this name "as a seal on his heart."

3. God's name is venerable. Thus, the Apostle says, "At the name of Jesus every knee should bow, of things in heaven, on earth, and under the earth."[92] *Of things in heaven* refers to the angels and the blessed; *of things on earth* refers to the inhabitants of the earth, who bow for love of the heaven which they desire to obtain; and *of things under the earth* refers to the damned, who do so out of fear.

4. God's name is ineffable, because no tongue can describe it, for which reason sometimes it is explained with reference to created things. God's name is compared to *a rock* by reason of its stability: "On this rock I will build my church"[93]; *to fire*, because of its power to cleanse, since just as fire cleanses denser metals, so does God purify the hearts of sinners: "Thy God is a consuming fire"[94]; and *to light*, by reason of its enlightenment, for just as light banishes darkness, so the name of God banishes darkness from the mind: "My God, enlighten Thou my darkness."[95]

B. The meaning of *hallowed*
We pray then that this name be made manifest, that it may be known and hallowed. Now the Latin word *sanctum* ("holy" or "hallowed")

admits of a threefold meaning:

1. "Firm": *Sanctum* ["hallowed"] is the same as *sancitum* ("firm"). Thus, all the blessed in heaven are called saints, because they are firmly established in eternal bliss; but no one is a saint on earth, where all are continually changeable: "I sank away from Thee, and I wandered too much astray from Thee, my support."[96]

2. "The opposite of earthly" (i.e., "the opposite of sinners"): *Sanctum* ["hallowed"] may be rendered "unearthly." The saints in heaven have no earthly affections. Thus the Apostle says, "I count all things but as dung, that I may gain Christ."[97]

Earth signifies "sinners":

a. As regards production, since if the earth is not cultivated, it brings forth thorns and thistles. In like manner, the sinner's soul, unless it is cultivated by grace, brings forth nothing but the thistles and pricks of sins: "Thorns and thistles shall it bring forth to thee."[98]

b. As regards darkness, since the earth is dark and opaque as the sinner is dark and opaque: "Darkness was on the face of the abyss."[99]

c. As regards aridity, because earth as a dry element will not cohere without moisture to bind it together. So God placed the earth above the waters,[100] because the moisture of the waters holds together the arid and dry earth. In the same way, the sinner's soul is arid and devoid of humor: "My soul is as earth without water unto Thee."[101]

3. "Washed in blood": *Sanctum* ["hallowed"] may be understood as "washed in blood" (*sanguine tinctum*), since the saints in heaven are called saints because they have been washed in blood: "These are they who came out of great tribulation and have washed their robes… in the blood of the lamb."[102] And, "He hath washed us from our sins in His blood."[103]

V. THY KINGDOM COME (Second Petition)

A. The gift of piety

As already stated, the Holy Spirit makes us love, desire, and pray rightly. He begins by causing in us fear by which we ask that God's name be hallowed. Another gift of the Holy Spirit is *piety*.

Now piety, properly speaking, is a disposition of kindliness and devotion towards one's father, and towards all those who are in distress. Since God is our Father, as we have made evident, it follows that not only ought we to revere and fear Him, but we also ought to have a sweet and devout disposition towards Him. This makes us pray that His kingdom may come: "We should live righteously and piously in this present world, looking for the blessed hope and manifestation of the glory of the great God."[104]

B. Reasons for this petition

It may be asked, "Since the kingdom of God always was, why must we ask for it to come?" The answer may be understood in three ways:

1. So that all things may become subject to Him. Sometimes a king has only the *right* to a kingdom or throne, but as yet has not been proclaimed king because the inhabitants are not as yet subjected to him. In this sense, his kingdom or throne will come when those men are subject to him.

Now God by His very essence and nature is Lord of all. And Christ is Lord of all (not only as God, but as man by reason of His Godhead): "He gave Him power and glory and a kingdom."[105] Consequently, all things ought to be subject to Him. However, they are not subject as yet, but will be at the end of the world: "He must reign until He hath put all His enemies under His feet."[106] Therefore, it is for this that we pray when we say, *Thy kingdom come.*

In making this petition, we have a threefold purpose: a) the safeguarding of the just; b) the punishment of the wicked; and c) the destruction of death.

a. The safeguarding of the just. Man is subject to Christ in two ways, either willingly or unwillingly. Since God's will is efficacious, it must be fulfilled outright; and since God wills all things to be subject to Christ, one of two things is necessary: either that men do the will of God by submitting to His commandments (as the just do) or else that God wreak His will on men by punishing them (as He will do on sinners and on His enemies at the end of the world): "Until I make thy enemies thy footstool."[107] For these reasons, the saints are enjoined to ask that God's kingdom may come (i.e., that they may be wholly subject to Him).

b. The punishment of the wicked. To sinners, this is repellent, since their asking that God's kingdom may come is nothing less than their praying that by God's will they may be condemned to punishment: "Woe to them that desire the day of the Lord."[108]

c. The destruction of death. The result [of the coming of the kingdom] will be the destruction of death. Since Christ is life, in His kingdom there can be no death since it is contrary to life. Thus, it is said, "Last of all, the enemy, death, shall be destroyed."[109] This will be fulfilled at the resurrection: "He will transform the body of our lowliness, that it may be made like to the body of His glory."[110]

2. Because kingdom signifies the glory of paradise. We pray *Thy kingdom come* because the kingdom of heaven signifies the glory of paradise. This is easily understood. *Regnum* ("kingdom") is just another word for *regimen* ("government") and the best government is one in which nothing is done against the will of the governor. Now, since God wills men to be saved, God's will is the salvation of mankind,[111] which will be realized most especially in paradise where there will be nothing contrary to man's salvation: "They shall gather out of His kingdom all scandals."[112] In this world, however, there are many things contrary to the salvation of mankind. When, therefore, we pray *Thy kingdom come*, we ask to be made partakers of the heavenly kingdom and of the glory of paradise.

Moreover, this kingdom is most desirable for three reasons:

a. Its supreme righteousness. It is desirable because of the supreme righteousness that obtains there: "Thy people shall be all righteous."[113] Here below the wicked are mingled with the good, whereas in heaven there are no wicked and no sinners.

b. Its perfect liberty. This kingdom is desirable because of its perfect liberty. Although all men desire liberty naturally, here there is none; but in heaven there is perfect liberty without any trace of bondage: "The creature itself will be delivered from the slavery of corruption."[114]

In fact, not only will all be free, but all will be kings: "Thou hast made us to our God a kingdom."[115] This is because all shall be of one will with God: whatever the saints will, God shall will; and whatever God wills, the saints shall will. Therefore, their will shall be done with God's will. In this way, all will reign, since the will of all will be done, and God shall be the crown of all: "In that day shall the Lord of hosts be for a crown of glory and for a diadem of beauty unto the residue of His people."[116]

c. Its wondrous wealth. This kingdom is also desirable because of its wondrous wealth: "The eye hath not seen, O God, besides Thee, what things Thou hast prepared for them that wait on Thee."[117] "Who satisfieth thy desire with good things."[118]

Take note that whatever man seeks in this world, he will find it more perfect and more excellent in God alone.[119] If you seek delight, you will find supreme delight in God: "You shall see and your heart shall rejoice."[120] "And everlasting joy shall be upon their heads."[121] Do you seek wealth? You will find in Him all things you desire in abundance: "When the soul strays from Thee she seeks things apart from Thee, but finds all things impure and unprofitable until she returns to Thee."[122]

3. Because sometimes sin reigns in this world. We pray *Thy kingdom come* because sometimes sin reigns in this world. This occurs when a man is so disposed that he follows at once the lure of sin and carries it into effect: "Let not sin reign in your mortal body"[123] but let God reign in your heart ("who says to Zion, 'Thy God shall reign'"[124]).

This will be when you are ready to obey God and keep all His commandments. When, therefore, we ask that His kingdom come, we pray that God (and not sin) may reign in us.

C. This fulfills the beatitude: "Blessed are the meek"

Thus, by this petition we shall obtain that beatitude[125] of which it is said: "Blessed are the meek."[126]

1. Reliance on God. According to the first explanation above [regarding our prayer that all may become subject to God], from the moment that a man desires God to be the Lord of all, he ceases to seek revenge for the injury done to himself and leaves that to God. For if you were to avenge yourself, you would no longer seek the advent of His kingdom.

2. Detachment from earthly goods. According to the second explanation above [regarding heaven as the reign of God in the glory of paradise], if you await the coming of His kingdom, i.e., the glory of paradise, you have no need to regret the loss of earthly goods.

3. Meekness. And according to the third explanation above [regarding the reign of sin in this world], if you pray that God may reign in you, Christ, Who was most meek, also will reign in you; and you will be meek in consequence: "Learn of me, for I am meek."[127] "Yet took joyfully the spoiling of your goods."[128]

VI. THY WILL BE DONE ON EARTH AS IT IS IN HEAVEN (Third Petition)
A. The gift of knowledge
Knowledge is the third gift bestowed on us by the Holy Spirit. For He bestows on the righteous not only the gift of fear and the gift of piety (which is a filial affection towards God, as already stated), but He also gives them wisdom. It is for this that David prayed: Teach me goodness, discipline, and knowledge."[129] By this knowledge the Holy Spirit teaches us how to lead a good life.

Now of all the signs of a man's knowledge and wisdom, none is proof of greater wisdom than that a man does not cling to his own opinion: "Lean not upon thine own prudence."[130] For those who cling to their own judgment so as to mistrust others and trust in themselves alone, invariably prove themselves fools and are judged as such. "Seest thou a man wise in his own conceit? There is more hope for a fool than for him."[131] But if a man distrusts his own judgment, that is a proof of his humility (which is why it is said, "Where humility is, there also is wisdom")[132] whereas the proud are too self-confident.

Accordingly, we learn from the Holy Spirit (by His gift of knowledge) to do not our own but God's will, and by virtue of this gift we pray to God that His will may be done on earth as it is in heaven. It is in this that the gift of knowledge is proved, so that when we say to God, *Thy will be done*, it is as when a sick man consults a physician. He takes the medicine not precisely because he wills it himself, but because it is the will of the physician. If he only took what he willed himself, he would be a fool.

Hence, we should ask nothing of God but that His will be done in our regard (in other words, that His will be fulfilled in us). For man's heart is right when it agrees with the divine will. Christ did this : "I came down from heaven to do, not my own will, but the will of Him that sent me."[133] For as God, Christ has the same will as the Father; but as man, He has a distinct will from the Father and in respect of this will, He says that He does not His own but His Father's will. For that reason, He taught us to ask and pray, *Thy will be done*.

But how can this be explained in the face of the words of the Psalm: "He hath done whatsoever he hath willed"?[134] If he has done whatever He pleased in heaven and on earth, what does He mean when He makes us say, *Thy will be done on earth as it is in heaven?*

B. God's will for us

This is explained by observing that God wills three things in our regard, which we pray to be fulfilled:

1. Eternal life. God wills that we may have eternal life, because whoever makes a certain thing for a certain purpose wills that purpose for it. God made man, but not without a purpose, for as the Psalm says, "Hast Thou made all the children of men in vain?"[135] Therefore, He made man for a certain purpose; but not for the sake of material pleasures, since dumb animals have them, but that he may have eternal life. For it is the Lord's will that man have eternal life.

When a thing attains the end for which it was made it is said to be saved, whereas when it fails to reach that end, it is said to be lost. Now God made man for eternal life; and consequently, when man obtains eternal life, he is saved, which is God's will: "This is the will of my Father Who sent me, that whosoever beholdeth the Son and believeth in Him, have eternal life."[136] This will is already fulfilled in angels and saints, who are in heaven, who see, know, and enjoy God.

But we desire that as God's will is fulfilled in the blessed who are in heaven, even so may it be fulfilled in us who are on earth. This, then, is the sense of our prayer, *Thy will be done:* namely, that it be done in us who are on earth, even as it is fulfilled in the saints who are in heaven.

2. Obedience to the commandments. God wills that we keep His commandments, because when we desire a particular thing, we do not only will what we desire, but we also will whatever enables us to obtain it. Thus, a physician, in order to restore a man to health, also wills his diet, his medicine, and so on. Now God wills us to obtain eternal life: "If thou wouldst enter life, keep the commandments."[137]

Therefore, He wills us to keep the commandments: "Your reasonable service... so that ye find out what is the *good* and the *well-pleasing* and the *perfect* will of God."[138]

a. God's will is good: "Who teaches thee to profit."[139]

b. God's will is well-pleasing, and though displeasing to others, yet delightful to those who love His will: "Light is risen for the righteous and joy for the upright in heart."[140]

c. God's will is perfect: "Be ye perfect as also your heavenly Father is perfect."[141]

So when we say, *Thy will be done,* we pray that we may keep God's commandments; and this will of God is fulfilled in the righteous, but is not yet fulfilled in sinners. Now the righteous are signified by *heaven* and sinners by *earth.* Hence we pray that God's will be done on *earth,* i.e., in sinners, even as it is done in *heaven*, i.e., in the righteous.

We must observe here that we have something to learn from the very manner of expression. For He does not say *Do* or *Let us do* but *Thy will be done*. This is because two things are required in order to obtain eternal life: the grace of God and man's will. And although God made man without man's help, He does not sanctify him without his cooperation. As Augustine says, "He Who created thee without thyself, will not justify thee without thyself,"[142] because He wishes man to cooperate: "Turn ye unto me and I will turn unto you."[143] "By the grace of God I am what I am, and His grace in me hath not been void."[144] Presume not therefore on yourself, but trust in the grace of God; nor be neglectful, but do your utmost.

Hence Christ does not say, *Let us do* (lest He seem to imply that God's grace counts for nothing); nor does He say, *Do* (lest He seem to state that man's will and effort are of no account). Rather he says, *Be it done* — by God's grace, with solicitude and effort on our part.

3. Restoration of the original dignity of man. God wills that man be restored to the state and dignity in which the first man was created, which was so great that his spirit and soul experienced no rebellion on the part of his flesh and sensuality. For as long as the soul was subject to God, the flesh was so subject to the spirit that it felt no corruption, whether of death or of sickness or of other passions.

But from the moment that the spirit and soul that stood between God and the flesh rebelled against God by sin, there and then the body rebelled against the soul. It began to be aware of death and infirmity, as well as of the ceaseless rebellion of sensuality against the spirit: "I behold another law in my members, warring against the law of my mind."[145] "The flesh lusteth against the spirit and the spirit against the flesh."[146]

Thus, there is continual war between flesh and spirit, and man is ever being worsened by sin. Hence, it is God's will that man be restored to his pristine state, namely that the flesh be wholly delivered from all that rebels against the spirit: "This is the will of God, your sanctification."[147]

But this will of God cannot be fulfilled in this life, whereas it will be fulfilled at the resurrection of the saints, when bodies will arise in glory and incorruption, and in a state of great perfection: "It is sown in dishonor; it shall rise in glory."[148] In the righteous, however, God's will is fulfilled with regard to the spirit by their righteousness, knowledge, and life. And therefore, when we say, *Thy will be done*, we pray that this may be fulfilled also in the flesh. In this way, we take *heaven* to signify the spirit and *earth* to indicate the flesh. So the sense is, *Thy will be done* on *earth* (i.e., in our flesh) *as it is done in heaven* (i.e., in our spirit) by righteousness.

C. This fulfills the beatitude: "Blessed are they who mourn"

By this petition, we reach the blessedness of those who mourn, of which it is said: "Blessed are they who mourn, for they shall be comforted."[149] This applies to each of the three explanations given above:

1. Because eternal life is delayed. In accordance with the first explanation (above), we mourn because we desire eternal life, but it is delayed: "Woe is me that my sojourn is prolonged."[150] In fact, in the saints this longing is so great that because of it, they desire death which in itself is repellent: "We have the courage even to prefer to be exiled from the body and to be at home with the Lord."[151]

2. Because keeping the commandments is painful. In accordance with the second explanation (above), we mourn because we desire to keep the commandments, yet, however sweet the commandments are to the soul, they are bitter to the flesh, which is continually buffeted: in the flesh, "going they went and wept." but in the soul, "coming they shall come with joy."[152]

3. Because flesh and spirit conflict. In accordance with the third explanation (above), we mourn because of the continual conflict between our flesh and our spirit [which frustrates our desire to be restored to the dignity of the first man], yet it is impossible for the soul not to be wounded at least by venial sins due to the flesh. This is why, until the soul is healed, it mourns: "Every night" (i.e., in the darkness of sin) "I will wash my bed" (i.e., my conscience).[153]

And they who weep thus reach their heavenly country, *to which may God bring us all.*

VII. GIVE US THIS DAY OUR DAILY BREAD
(Fourth Petition)
A. The gift of fortitude

It often happens that one who is given great knowledge and wisdom is for that very reason disheartened, and so needs fortitude to hearten him lest he lack necessities. "It is He that giveth strength to the weary and increaseth force and might to them that are not."[154] It is the Holy Spirit Who gives this fortitude: "The Spirit entered into me… and He set me upon my feet."[155] And this gift of fortitude prevents man's heart from fainting through fear of lacking necessities, and makes him trust without wavering that God will provide him with whatever he needs. For this reason, the Holy Spirit, the giver of this fortitude, teaches us to pray to God *to give us this day our daily bread.* For this reason, He is called the "Spirit of Fortitude."[156]

Observe here that in the first three petitions, we ask for spiritual blessings that are begun in this life here below but are not perfected except in eternal life. So when we pray that God's name be hallowed, we ask that God's holiness be made known; when we pray that His kingdom may come, we ask that we be made partakers of eternal life; and when we pray that His will be done, we ask that His will be fulfilled in us.

Although all these petitions begin to be fulfilled here below, they cannot be realized perfectly except in eternal life. Consequently, we need to pray for certain necessary things which can be had perfectly in the present life, and for this reason the Holy Spirit has taught us to ask for the needs of this present life. With these needs it is possible to be supplied perfectly here below, indicating at the same time that it is God Who provides us with temporal goods. This is signified in the words, *Give us this day our daily bread.*

B. Sins that arise from desiring temporal goods

In these same words the Holy Spirit teaches us to avoid the sins which tend to arise from the desire for temporal goods:

1. Greed. The first is unbridled greed, whereby a man seeks things above his station and condition of life, being dissatisfied with those in keeping with it. For instance, if he is a common soldier, he wants to dress not as a soldier but as a nobleman; if he is an ordinary clergyman, he wishes to clothe himself not as a cleric but as a bishop. This vice draws a man away from spiritual goods, insofar as it makes him have an overwhelming desire for temporal things.

Our Lord taught us to shun this vice by praying for bread only, i.e., the needs of the present life, each one according to his own station, which needs are expressed under the name of *bread*. Hence, He did not teach us to ask for uncommon things, luxurious things, or a variety of things, but for bread without which man cannot live, since it is the common need of all: "The chief thing for man's life is water and bread."[157] "Having food and clothing, with these we shall be content.."[158]

2. Fraud. The second vice consists in molesting and defrauding others in the acquisition of temporal good. This vice is all the more fraught with danger since it is difficult to restore ill-gotten goods. For according to Augustine, "unless a man restores what he has purloined, his sin is not forgiven."[159] Accordingly, we are taught here to shun this vice by asking for our own and not another's bread (since robbers eat not their own bread but another's).

3. Excessive solicitude. There are some who are never satisfied with what they have and always want more. This is lack of moderation, since desire should always be measured according to one's needs: "Give me neither beggary nor riches; give me but the necessities of life."[160] We are warned to avoid this vice in the words, *our daily bread*, that is to say, *the bread for one day or for one season.*

4. Voraciousness. This is the vice whereby some would devour in one day what would suffice for several days. These seek bread not for today but for ten days and through being overly lavish they waste all of it: "The drunkard and the glutton shall come to beggary."[161] "A workman that is a drunkard shall not be rich."[162]

5. Ingratitude. This is a great evil, since the ungrateful man prides himself on his wealth and fails to acknowledge that he owes all to God.

Whatever we have, be it spiritual or temporal, comes from God: "All things are Thine and of Thine own have we given Thee."[163] Hence, in order to remove this vice, the Lord even says, *"Give us our daily bread,* to remind us that all we have comes from God.

From this we learn a lesson. Sometimes a man has great wealth but derives no benefit from it, instead incurring loss both spiritual and temporal. Some have perished through riches: "There is also another grievous evil which I have seen under the sun and that is common among men: a man to whom God hath given riches, wealth, and honor, so that his soul wanteth nothing at all that he desireth, yet God giveth him not power to eat thereof, but a stranger eateth it up."[164] And again: "Riches gathered together to the hurt of the owner."[165]

For this reason, we ought to pray that we may derive benefit from our wealth; and this we pray for when we say, *give us our bread,* i.e., make our wealth profitable to us: "His bread in his belly shall be turned into the gall of asps within him. The riches which he hath swallowed he shall vomit up; God shall draw them out of his belly."[166]

6. Concern for worldly possessions. There are some who are worried from day to day about temporal matters as much as a year in advance. Those who are so concerned are never at rest: "Be not solicitous, saying: 'What shall we eat?' or 'What shall we drink?' or 'What are we to put on?'"[167] Hence, our Lord teaches us to ask that our bread be given us *today,* i.e., whatever we need for the present.

C. The twofold meaning of *bread*
Moreover, we may discover in this bread another twofold meaning: the Sacramental Bread and the Bread of God's Word.

1. Sacramental bread. Thus, we ask for our Sacramental Bread which is prepared for us every day in the Church, praying that as we receive it sacramentally, so may it profit us unto salvation: "I am the living bread which came down from heaven."[168] "He that eateth and drinketh unworthily eateth and drinketh judgment to himself."[169]

2. The Word of God. Again, this bread means the Word of God: "Not by bread alone doth man live but by every word that proceedeth from the mouth of God."[170] Hence, we pray to Him to give us bread, that is to say, His Word. From this there arises in man the beatitude of hungering for righteousness, because the possession of spiritual goods increases our desire for them. This desire begets that hunger whose reward is the fullness of eternal life.

VIII. AND FORGIVE US OUR TRESPASSES AS WE FORGIVE THOSE WHO TRESPASS AGAINST US\
(Fifth Petition)
A. The gift of counsel
There are, indeed, some possessed of great wisdom and fortitude who yet, being overconfident of their own powers, do not act wisely nor do they succeed in accomplishing what they intend: "Purpose is strengthened by counsel."[171] We must observe, however, that the Holy Spirit Who gives strength also gives counsel, for every good counsel in the matter of man's spiritual welfare comes from the Holy Spirit.

Now, man needs counsel when he is in trouble, just as he needs to consult a physician when he is sick. So when his soul is sick through sin, he must seek counsel in order to be healed. That the sinner needs counsel is indicated in the words of Daniel: "Let my counsel be acceptable unto thee, O King, and redeem thou thy sins with alms."[172] Hence, it is a very good counsel against sin that a man give alms and show mercy. For this reason, the Holy Spirit teaches sinners to make this petition and to pray, *forgive us our trespasses.*

We owe God that which we take away from His right, and God's right is that we do His will in preference to our own. Hence, we deprive God of His right when we prefer our own will to His, and this is sin. Therefore, sins are our debts, and the Holy Spirit counsels us to ask forgiveness of our sins. For this reason, we say, *forgive us our trespasses* [literally, *debts*].

Regarding these words, we may consider the following points: a) Why do we make this petition?, b) When is it fulfilled?, and c) What is required of us that it may be fulfilled?

B. Reasons for asking forgiveness
From this petition we gather two things that we need in this life:

1. That we may be ever fearful and humble, for there have been some so presumptuous as to assert that it is possible for man by his own powers to live here below without committing sin. But this has been given to none except Christ (Who had the Spirit without measure) and the Blessed Virgin (who was full of grace, in whom there was no sin, and "of whom," Augustine says, "in the matter of sin, it is my wish to exclude all mention whatsoever."[173])

To no other saint has this been granted without their incurring at least venial sin: "If we say that we have not sin, we deceive ourselves, and the truth is not in us."[174] This is confirmed by this fifth petition, for we cannot doubt that it is proper even for holy men to recite the *Our Father*, which includes the petition, *Forgive us our trespasses*; and, therefore, all acknowledge and confess themselves to be sinners or debtors. If, then, you are a sinner, you must be fearful and humble yourself.

2. That we should ever live in hope, for even though we are sinners, we must not despair, lest despair lead us to various and greater sins. Thus, the Apostle says, "Who despairing have given themselves over to licentiousness, unto the working of all uncleanness."[175] It is, therefore, most profitable for us to hope always, since however great a sinner a man may be, he should hope that God will forgive him if he is thoroughly contrite and converted. This hope is strengthened in us when we pray, *Forgive us our trespasses*.

The Novatians, however, destroyed this hope, for they said that those who sin once after being baptized never receive mercy. But this is not true, if Christ spoke the truth when He said, "I forgave thee all the debt because thou besoughtest me."[176] Consequently, whenever you ask for mercy you shall receive it, provided you ask with repentance for your sin.

Accordingly, this petition gives rise to fear and hope, because every sinner who is contrite and confesses his sin receives mercy: and hence the need of this petition.

C. When is this petition fulfilled?
As regards the second point, we must observe that in sin there are two factors: the fault by which God is offended and the punishment due to the fault. The fault, however, is remitted through contrition which includes the intention of amendment and atonement: "I said, I will confess my

transgressions unto the Lord; and Thou forgavest the iniquity of my sin."[177] Hence, man must not despair, seeing that contrition together with the intention of confessing suffices for the forgiveness of sin.

Possibly someone will object, "If sins are forgiven when a man is contrite, why does he need a priest?" I reply that in contrition, God forgives the fault and commutes eternal punishment into temporal; but the debt of temporal punishment remains.[178] Hence, if man were to die without confession — not because he refused it, but through being prevented — he would go to purgatory, the punishment of which is very great, as Augustine says.

Accordingly, when you confess your sin, the priest absolves you from this punishment by the power of the keys to which you have submitted in confession. For this reason, Christ said to His apostles, "Receive ye the Holy Spirit; whose sins ye shall forgive, they are forgiven them; and whose sins ye shall retain, they are retained.[179] Hence, if a man confesses once, some part of this punishment is taken away, and likewise when he confesses a second time. In fact, it may be that he confesses the sin so often that the whole punishment is remitted.

Moreover, the successors of the Apostles devised another means for the remission of this punishment, namely, the granting of indulgences[180] which avail those who are in a state of grace as much as is claimed for them and as indicated by the grantor. That the Pope can do this is sufficiently clear. For many are the good deeds of holy men who have never sinned, at least not mortally, which deeds were done for the common good of the Church. Likewise, the merits of Christ, and those of the Blessed Virgin are, as it were, the treasury of the Church. Thus, the sovereign pontiff and those whom he delegates for the purpose, can allocate these merits whenever the need occurs. Consequently, sins are remitted not only as to their guilt by contrition, but also as to their punishment by confession and by indulgences.

D. What is required of us?

As regards the third point, we must observe that on our part we must forgive our neighbor his offenses against us, which is why it is added, *as we forgive those who trespass against us.* Otherwise, God would not forgive us: "man to man reserveth anger; and doth he seek remedy of God?"[181] "Forgive and you shall be forgiven."[182] Thus, this petition alone is made conditional, by our saying, *as we forgive those who trespass against us.* For if you do not forgive, you will not be forgiven.

You might say, "I will say the first part (*forgive us*) but I will omit what follows (*as we forgive those who trespass against us*)." Do you then seek to deceive Christ? Be sure that you do no such thing, since Christ Who made this prayer remembers it well, and therefore He cannot be deceived. If, therefore, you say the words with your lips, fulfill them in your heart.

But someone may ask whether one who does not intend to forgive his neighbor, ought to say, *as we forgive those who trespass against us.* It seems not, since his words would be a lie. I answer that he does not lie, for he does not pray in his own person, but in that of the Church, who is not deceived; hence, the petition is expressed in the plural.

Observe, however, that forgiveness is twofold. There is the forgiveness of those who are perfect, when he who is offended seeks out the offender: "Seek peace."[183] The other forgiveness applies to all in general, namely that we forgive those who ask to be forgiven: "Forgive thy neighbor if he hath hurt thee, and then shall thy sins be forgiven thee when thou prayest."[184]

This leads us to another beatitude: *Blessed are the merciful,* for mercifulness makes us show mercy to our neighbor.

IX. AND LEAD US NOT INTO TEMPTATION
(Sixth Petition)

Some, although they have sinned, desire forgiveness of their sins and for this reason confess them and repent — yet they do not strive as much as they ought in order not to sin again. In this they are inconsistent: on the one hand they deplore their sins by repenting of them, while on the other hand, by sinning again, they have more sins to deplore. Thus we read, "Wash yourselves, make yourselves clean, take away the evil of your devices from before my eyes, cease to do evil."[185] Hence, as stated above, Christ in the foregoing petition taught us to ask that we may be able to avoid sin — that is, that we be not led into temptation and thus fall into sin: *And lead us not into temptation.*

Three questions arise here: a) What is temptation?, b) How and by whom is man tempted?, and c) How is he freed from temptation?

A. The nature of temptation

To tempt is nothing else but to try or to prove, so that to tempt a man is to prove his virtue.[186] Now, a man's virtue is tried or proven in two ways, corresponding to two things required by it. One requirement concerns doing good, in that virtue enables him to do good deeds; the other requirement is that he avoid evil: "Depart from evil and do good."[187] Accordingly, a man's virtue is tried sometimes as regards his doing good, sometimes as regards his avoiding evil:

1. Regarding the doing of good. A man is sometimes tried in his readiness to do good deeds (for instance, to fast and the like) because your virtue is great when you are ready to do good. Thus, God sometimes tempts a man, not that the man's virtue is unknown to Him, but that all may know it and take it as an example. In this way, God tempted Abraham[188] and Job,[189] and it is thus that He often sends trials to the righteous, in order that by bearing trials in patience their virtue may be made manifest and they may themselves advance in virtue: "The Lord your God proveth you, that it may appear whether or not ye love Him."[190] Thus, God tempts man by inciting him to good deeds.

2. Regarding the doing of evil. A man's virtue is also tried by inducing him to evil deeds. If he offers strong resistance and does not consent, his virtue is great; whereas, if he yields to the temptation, he is devoid of virtue. In this way, no man is tempted by God, for as it is said, "God cannot be tempted to evil things; and Himself tempteth no man."[191]

B. The sources of temptation

Man is tempted by his own flesh, by the devil, and by the world:

1. The flesh tempts man in two ways:

   a. The flesh instigates man to evil, since it always seeks its own gratification, namely carnal pleasures in which sin often occurs. For a man who indulges in carnal pleasures neglects spiritual things: "Everyone is tempted… by his own lust."[192]

   b. The flesh entices man from good, for the spirit, for its own part, would always delight in spiritual goods, but the flesh encumbers and hinders the spirit: "The corruptible body is a load upon the soul."[193] "I delight in the law of God after the inward man, but I behold another law in my members, warring against the law of my mind and making me a captive to the law of sin which is in my members."[194] This temptation that comes from the flesh is most grievous since our foe, the flesh, is united to us; and as Boethius says, "No plague is more harmful than an enemy in the household." Therefore, we must be on the watch against it: "Watch and pray lest ye enter into temptation."[195]

2. The devil tempts man with very great force, for even when the flesh is subdued, another tempter arises, namely, the devil, against whom we have a mighty struggle. Hence, the Apostle says, "Our wrestling is not against flesh and blood, but against principalities, against the powers, against the world-rulers of this darkness."[196] For this reason, he is called significantly the Tempter: "Lest haply the tempter hath tempted you."[197] In tempting he proceeds most cunningly. Like a skillful general about to besiege a fortified city, he seeks out the weak points in the object of his assault and tempts a man in those things in which he sees him to be weak. For this reason, he tempts him in those sins to which, after subduing his flesh, man is most inclined (for instance, to anger, pride, and other spiritual sins): "Your adversary the devil goeth about as a roaring lion seeking to devour."[198]

The devil tempts man in two ways:

a. The devil deceives man: He does not at once suggest to man something that has an appearance of evil, but something that has a semblance of good. Thereby, at least in the beginning, he turns man from his chief purpose; afterwards, it becomes easier for him to induce man to sin, once man has been turned ever so little from the purpose: "Even Satan disguiseth himself as an angel of light."[199]

b. The devil enthralls man in his sin: Having led man on to sin, the devil so enthralls him as to prevent him from arising out of sin: "The sinews of his testicles are wrapped together."[200] The devil, then, does two things: he deceives a man and after deceiving him, enchains him in his sin.

3. The world tempts man in two ways:

    a. By awakening a desire for earthly goods. The world tempts man by awakening in him an excessive and unbridled desire for earthly goods. For this reason, the Apostle says that "the love of money is the root of all evils."[201]

    b. By threatening him with persecution. The world also tempts man by the threats of persecutors and tyrants: "We are wrapped up in darkness."[202] "All that would live piously in Christ Jesus shall suffer persecution."[203] "Fear not those that slay the body."[204]

Accordingly, it is now clear what temptation is and in what way and by whom man is tempted. We now have to see how man is to be freed from temptation.

C. Release from temptation

Here we must observe that Christ teaches us to pray, not that we may not be tempted but that we may not be *led into temptation* — for if man overcomes temptation, he deserves a crown. Hence, it is said, "Deem it all delight my brethren, when ye fall into diverse temptations"[205] and "Son, when thou comest to the service of God... prepare thy soul for temptation."[206] Again: "Blessed is the man that is patient under temptation, for when he hath been proved he shall receive the crown of life."[207] Hence, Christ teaches us to pray that we not be led into temptation by consenting to it. "Temptation hath not come upon you but such as man can bear,"[208] because to be tempted is human, but to consent is devilish.

But does God lead a man to evil, so that we should say, *And lead us not into temptation?* I reply that God is said to lead us to evil by permitting us to do evil, to the extent that He withdraws His grace[209] from man by reason of his many sins, in consequence of which man falls into sin. For this reason, we chant, "Forsake me not, O Lord, when my strength faileth."[210]

Yet He guides man by the fervor of charity, lest man be led into temptation, for the very least degree of charity is able to resist any sin whatever: "Many waters cannot quench charity."[211]

He also guides us by the light of our intelligence, by which He teaches us what to do. For, as the Philosopher says, everyone who sins is ignorant.[212]

Thus, we read, "I will give thee understanding and will instruct thee."[213] For this David prayed when he said, "Enlighten mine eyes lest I sleep in death; lest mine enemy say, I have prevailed against him."[214] This is imparted to us in the gift of understanding. Thus, when we do not consent to temptation, we keep our hearts clean, of which it is said: "Blessed are the clean of heart, for they shall see God."[215]

It follows from this that this petition brings us to the sight of God, *to which may God lead us all.*

X. BUT DELIVER US FROM EVIL
(Seventh Petition)

In the foregoing petitions, our Lord teaches us to seek forgiveness of our sins and how we may avoid temptations. In this petition, He bids us pray to be safeguarded from evils. This is a general petition against all evils (namely sins, sickness, and afflictions, as Augustine says). Seeing, however, that mention has already been made of sin and temptation, it remains for other evils to be mentioned (namely, the trials and afflictions of this world) from which God delivers us in four ways:

A. God prevents evils

God prevents the occurrence of evils, but He does not do this often, since the saints are afflicted in this world and since "everyone who would live piously in Christ Jesus shall suffer persecution."[216] Yet, sometimes God does prevent a man from being afflicted by an evil — namely when He knows him to be unable to bear it (just as a physician does not apply violent remedies to a weak patient): "Behold, I have set before thee an open door, and no man can shut it, for thou hast little strength."[217] In heaven, however, this will apply to all, seeing that there none will be afflicted: "He shall deliver thee in six troubles" (those, that is, of the present life, which is divided into six stages) "and in the seventh, evil shall not touch thee."[218] "They shall hunger no more, neither thirst any more."[219]

B. God comforts the suffering

He delivers us from afflictions when He comforts us in them. For unless He comforts us, we cannot endure: "We were utterly weighted down beyond our strength."[220] "God, Who comforteth the humble, comforteth us."[221] "According to the multitude of my sorrows in my heart, Thy comforts delight my soul."[222]

C. God rewards the afflicted

He bestows so many blessings on those who are afflicted that their evils are forgotten: "After the storm, Thou makest it calm."[223] Hence, such afflictions and trials are not to be feared, since they are easy to bear both on account of the attendant consolations and because of their short duration: "Our present light affliction ever more and more abundantly worketh out for us an eternal weight of glory,"[224] because by means thereof we obtain eternal life.

D. God strengtens man through trials

He delivers us from evil insofar as temptations and trials are conducive to our profit. Thus, He does not say, *Deliver us from trials*, but *from evil*, because trials bring the saints a crown, and for that reason they glory in their trials. Thus, the Apostle says, "And not only so, but we exult in our tribulations also, knowing that tribulation worketh patience."[225] "In time of tribulation, Thou forgivest sins."[226]

Thus, God delivers man from evil and from trials by turning them to man's profit, which is a sign of very great wisdom, because it is a mark of wisdom to direct evil to a good purpose (and this is the result of patience in bearing trials).

Other virtues, indeed, employ good things, but patience profits by evil things, which is why it is necessary only in evils, i.e., in adversity: "The learning of a man is known by his patience."[227]

Hence, the Holy Spirit, by means of the gift of wisdom, makes us pray this way, so that we may obtain the beatitude which is the reward of peace. For by patience, we obtain peace whether times be good or evil. For this reason, peacemakers are called the children of God because they are like God: just as nothing can hurt God, so nothing can harm them, whether they prosper or suffer. Therefore, "Blessed are the peacemakers, for they shall be called the children of God."[228]

Amen. This is said to ratify all the petitions.

XI. A SHORT EXPOSITION OF THE WHOLE PRAYER

By way of summing up what has been said, observe that the Lord's

Prayer contains what we ought to desire and what we ought to avoid:[229]

A. What men should desire

1. The glory of God. Of all desirable things, the first place belongs to that which is most lovable. This is God, and therefore, you seek first the glory of God by saying, *Hallowed be Thy name.*

Concerning *yourself*, you should desire from God:

2. Eternal life. For this you pray by saying, *Thy kingdom come.*

3. Fulfillment of God's will and His justice. For this, you ask by saying, "*Thy will be done on earth as it is in heaven.*

4. The necessities of life. For this you pray by saying, *Give us this day our daily bread.*

Of these [things you should desire for yourself] our Lord says, "Seek ye first the kingdom of God" (as regard the first); "and His justice" (as regards the second); "and all these things shall be added unto you" (as regards the third).[230]

B. What men should avoid

The things to be avoided and fled from are those which are incompatible with the fourfold good (indicated above):

1. Evil, which cannot destroy the glory of God: "If thou sin, what shalt thou hurt Him? If thou be righteous, what givest thou Him?"[231] For the evil with which He punishes and the good with which He rewards resound to God's glory.

2. Sin, which is contrary to eternal life, because by sin, eternal life is lost. Therefore, to remove this evil we say, *Forgive us our trespasses as we forgive those who trespass against us.*

3. Temptations, which are opposed to righteousness and good works, since temptations hinder us from performing good works. To remove this evil, we pray, *And lead us not into temptation.*

4. Troubles and trials, which are opposed to all those goods that we need.

To remove these evils, we pray, *But deliver us from evil. Amen.*

A TREATISE ON THE LORD'S PRAYER

by Saint Cyprian, Bishop and Martyr

et Your Prayer Come From A Humble Heart
When we pray, our words should be calm, modest and disciplined. Let us reflect that we are standing before God. We should please him both by our bodily posture and the manner of our speech. It is characteristic of the vulgar to shout and make a noise, not those who are modest. On the contrary, they should employ a quiet tone in their prayer.

Moreover, in the course of His teaching, the Lord instructed us to pray in secret. Hidden and secluded places, even our own rooms, give witness to our belief that God is present everywhere; that He sees and hears all; that in the fullness of his majesty, he penetrates hidden and secret places. This is the teaching of Jeremiah: *Am I God when I am near, and not God when I am far away? Can anyone hide in a dark corner without my seeing him? Do I not fill heaven and earth?* Another passage of Scripture says: *The eyes of the Lord are everywhere, observing both good and wicked men.*

The same modesty and discipline should characterize our liturgical prayer as well. When we gather to celebrate the divine mysteries with God's priest, we should not express our prayer in unruly words; the petition that should be made to God with moderation is not to be shouted out noisily and verbosely. For God hears our heart not our voice. He sees our thoughts; he is not to be shouted at. The Lord showed us this when he asked: *Why do you think evil in your hearts?* The book of Revelation testifies to this also: *And all the churches shall know that I am the one who searches the heart and the desires.*

Anna maintained this rule; in her observance of it, she is an image of the Church. In the First Book of Kings, we are told that she prayed quietly and modestly to God in the recesses of her heart.

Her prayer was secret, but her faith was evident. She did not pray with her voice, but with her heart, for she knew that in this way, the Lord would hear her. She prayed with faith and obtained what she sought. Scripture makes this clear in the words: *She was speaking in her heart; her lips were moving but her voice could not be heard; and the Lord heard her prayer.* The psalmist also reminds us: *Commune within your own hearts, and in the privacy of your room express your remorse.* This is the teaching of the Holy Spirit. Through Jeremiah, he suggests this: *Say in your hearts: Lord, it is You that we have to worship.*

My friends, anyone who worships should remember the way in which the tax-collector prayed in the temple alongside the Pharisee. He did not raise his eyes immodestly to heaven or lift up his hands arrogantly. Instead, he struck his breast and confessing the sins hidden within his heart, he implored the assistance of God's mercy. While the Pharisee was pleased with himself, the tax-collector deserved to be cleansed much more because of the manner in which he prayed. For he did not place his hope of salvation in the certainty of his own innocence; indeed, no one is innocent. Rather, he prayed humbly, confessing his sins. And the Lord, who forgives the lowly, heard his prayer.

Our Prayer Is Communal

Above all, he who preaches peace and unity did not want us to pray by ourselves in private or for ourselves alone. We do not say, "My Father, who art in heaven," nor "Give me this day my daily bread." It is not for himself alone that each person asks to be forgiven, not to be led into temptation or to be delivered from evil. Rather, we pray in public as a community, and not for one individual but for all. For the people of God are all one.

God is then the teacher of harmony, peace and unity, and desires each of us to pray for all men, even as he bore all men in himself alone. The three young men shut up in the furnace of fire observed this rule of prayer. United in the bond of the Spirit, they uttered together the same prayer. The witness of holy Scripture describes this incident for us, so that we might imitate them in our prayer. *Then all three began to sing in unison, blessing God.* Even though Christ had not yet taught them to pray, nevertheless, they spoke as with one voice.

It is for this reason that their prayer was persuasive and efficacious. For their simple and spiritual prayer of peace merited the presence of the Lord. So too, after the ascension, we find the apostles and the disciples praying together in this way. Scripture related: *They all joined together in continuous prayer, with the women including Mary, the mother of Jesus, and his brothers.* They all joined together in continuous prayer. The urgency and the unity of their prayer declares that God, *who fashions a bond of unity among those who live in his home,* will admit into his divine home for all eternity only those who pray in unity.

My dear friends, the Lord's Prayer contains many great mysteries of our faith. In these few words, there is great spiritual strength, for this summary of divine teaching contains all of our prayers and petitions. And so, the Lord commands us: *Pray then like this: Our Father, who art in heaven.*

We are new men; we have been reborn and restored to God by his grace. We have already begun to be his sons and we can say "Father." John reminds us of this: *He came to his own home, and his own people did not receive him. But to all who received him, who believe in his name, he gave the power to become children of God.* Profess your belief that you are sons of God by giving thanks. Call upon God who is your Father in heaven.

May Your Name Be Hallowed

How merciful the Lord is to us, how kind and richly compassionate! He wished us to repeat this prayer in God's sight, to call the Lord our Father and, as Christ is God's Son, be called in turn sons of God! None of us would ever have dared to utter this name unless he, himself, had allowed us to pray in this way. And therefore, dear friends, we should bear in mind and realize that when we call God our Father, we ought also to act like sons. If we are pleased to call Him Father, let Him in turn be pleased to call us sons.

We should live like the temples of God we are, so that it can be seen that God lives in us. No act of ours should be unworthy of the Spirit. Now that we have begun to live in heaven and in the Spirit, all our thoughts and actions should be heavenly and spiritual; for, as the Lord God himself has said, *Those who honor me I will honor, and those who despise me shall be despised.* And the blessed Apostle wrote in his letter, *You are not your own; you were bought with a great price. So glorify and bear God in your body.*

We go on to say, *May your name be hallowed.* It is not that we think to make God holy by our prayers; rather we are asking God that His name may be made holy in us. Indeed, how could God be made holy, he who is the source of holiness? Still, because he himself said, *Be holy, for I am holy,* we pray and beseech him that we who have been hallowed in baptism may persevere in what we have begun. And we pray for this every day, for we have need of daily sanctification; sinning every day, we cleanse our faults again and again by constant sanctification.

The apostle Paul instructs us in these words concerning the sanctification which God's loving kindness confers on us: *Neither the immoral, or idolaters, nor adulterers, nor homosexuals, nor thieves, nor the greedy, nor drunkards, nor revilers, nor robbers will inherit the kingdom of God. And such indeed you were. But you have been washed, you have been sanctified, you have been justified in the name of the Lord Jesus Christ and in the Spirit of our God.* We were sanctified, he says, *in the name of the Lord Jesus Christ and in the Spirit of our God.* Hence, we make our prayer that this sanctification may remain in us. But further, our Lord, who is also our judge, warns those who have been cured and brought back to life by him, to sin no more lest something worse happen to them. Thus, we offer constant prayers and beg night and day that this sanctification and new life which is ours by God's favor, be preserved by his protection.

Your Kingdom Come. Your Will Be Done.

The prayer continues: *Your kingdom come.* We pray that God's kingdom will become present for us in the same way that we ask for his name to be hallowed among us. For when does God not reign, when could there be in him a beginning of what always was and what will never cease to be? What we pray for is that the kingdom promised to us by God will come, the kingdom won by Christ's blood and passion. Then we who formerly were slaves in this world will reign from now on under the dominion of Christ, in accordance with his promise: *Come, O blessed of my Father, receive the kingdom which was prepared for you from the foundation of the world.*

However, my dear friends, it could also be that the kingdom of God whose coming we daily wish for is Christ himself, since it is his coming that we long for. He is our resurrection, since we rise again in him; so too he can be thought of as the kingdom of God because we are to reign in him. And it is good that we pray for God's kingdom; for though it is a heavenly kingdom, it is also an earthly one. But those who have already renounced the world are made greater by holding positions of authority in that kingdom.

After this we add: *Your will be done on earth as it is in heaven;* we pray not that God should do his will, but that we may carry out his will. How could anyone prevent the Lord from doing what he wills. But in our prayer, we ask that God's will be done in us because the devil throws up obstacles to prevent our mind and our conduct from obeying God in all things. So if his will is to be done in us, we have need of his will, that is, his help and protection. No one can be strong by his own strength or secure, save by God's mercy and forgiveness. Even the Lord, to show the weakness of the human nature which he bore, said: *Father, if it be possible, let this cup pass from me,* and then, by way of giving example to his disciples that they should do God's will and not their own, he added: *Nevertheless, not as I will, but as you will.*

All Christ did, all he taught, was the will of God. Humility in our daily lives, an unwavering faith, a moral sense of modesty in conversation, justice in act, mercy in deed, discipline, refusal to harm others, a readiness to suffer harm, peaceableness with our brothers, a wholehearted love of the Lord, loving in him what is of the Father, fearing him because he is God, preferring nothing to him who preferred nothing to us, clinging tenaciously to his love, standing by his cross with loyalty and courage whenever there is any conflict involving his honor and his name, manifesting in our speech the constancy of our profession and under torture confidence for the fight, and in dying the endurance for which we will be crowned — this is what it means to wish to be a co-heir with Christ, to keep God's command; this is what it means to do the will of the Father.

After the gift of bread we ask pardon for our sins

As the Lord's Prayer continues, we ask, *Give us this day our daily bread.* We can understand this petition in a spiritual and in a literal sense. For in the divine plan, both senses may help toward our salvation. For Christ is the bread of life; this bread does not belong to everyone, but is ours alone. When we say, *Our Father*, we understand that He is the Father of those who know Him and believe in Him. In the same way, we speak of our daily bread, because Christ is the bread of those who touch his body.

Now, we who live in Christ and receive his eucharist, the food of salvation, ask for this bread to be given us every day. Otherwise, we may be forced to abstain from this communion because of some serious sin. In this way, we shall be separated from the body of Christ, as he taught us in the words: *I am the bread of life which has come down from heaven. Anyone who eats my bread will live forever and the bread that I will give is my flesh for the life of the world.* Christ is saying, then, that anyone who eats his bread will live for ever. Clearly, they possess life who approach his body and share in the Eucharistic communion. For this reason, we should be apprehensive and pray that no one has to abstain from this communion, lest he be separated from the body of Christ and be far from salvation. Christ has warned of this: *If you do not eat the flesh of the Son of man and drink his blood you will have no life in you.* We pray for our daily bread, Christ, to be given to us. With his help, we who live and abide in him will never be separated from his body and his grace.

After this, we ask pardon for our sins, in the words: *and forgive us our trespasses.* The gift of bread is followed by a prayer for forgiveness. To be reminded that we are sinners and forced to ask forgiveness for our faults is prudent and sound. Even while we are asking God's forgiveness, our hearts are aware of our state! This command to pray daily for our sins reminds us that we commit sin every day. No one should complacently think himself innocent, lest his pride lead to further sin. Such is the warning that John gives us in his letter: *If we say we have no sin, we deceive ourselves, and the truth is not in us. If we confess our sins, the Lord is faithful and just, and will forgive our sins.* His letter includes both points, that we should beg for forgiveness for our sins, and that we receive pardon when we do. He calls the Lord faithful, because he remains loyal to his promise, by forgiving us our sins. He both taught us to pray for our sins and our faults, and also promised to show us a father's mercy and forgiveness.

We are God's children; let us abide in his peace

Christ clearly laid down an additional rule to bind us by a certain contractual condition: we ask that our debts be forgiven insofar as we forgive our own debtors. Thus, we are made aware that we cannot obtain what we ask regarding our own trespasses unless we do the same for those who trespass against us. This is why He says elsewhere: *The measure you give will be the measure you get.* And the servant who, after his master, forgives all his debt, refuses to forgive his fellow servant is thrown into prison. Because he refused to be kind to his fellow servant, he lost the favor his master had given him.

Along with his other precepts, Christ lays this down even more forcefully with a most vigorous condemnation. He says: *When you stand up to pray, if you have anything against anyone, let it go, so that your heavenly Father may also forgive you; but if you do not forgive men their trespasses, neither will your Father forgive you your trespasses.* You will have no excuse on the day of judgment, for then you will be judged just as you have judged, and you will suffer whatever you have done to others.

God bids us to be peace-loving, harmonious *and of one mind in his house;* he wants us to live with the new life he gave us at our second birth. As sons of God, we are to abide in peace; as we have one Spirit, we should be one in mind and heart. Thus, God does not receive the sacrifice of one who lives in conflict; and he orders us to turn back from the altar and be first reconciled with our brother, that God, too, may be appeased by the prayers of one who is at peace. The greatest offering we can make to God is our peace, harmony among fellow Christians, a people united with the unity of the Father, the Son and the Holy Spirit.

When Cain and Abel first offered their sacrifices, God considered not so much the gifts as the spirit of the giver: God was pleased with Abel's offering because he was pleased with his spirit. Thus, Abel the just man, the peacemaker, in his blameless sacrifice, taught men that when they offer their gift at the altar, they should approach as he did, in the fear of God, simplicity of heart, ruled by justice and peaceful harmony. Since this was the character of Abel's offering, it was only right that he himself should afterward become a sacrifice. As martyrdom's first witness and possessing the Lord's qualities of justice and peace, he foreshadowed the Lord's passion in the glory of his own death. Such, then, are the men who are crowned by the Lord and will be justified with him on the day of judgment.

But St. Paul and the sacred Scriptures tell us that the quarrelsome man and the troublemaker, who is never at peace with his brothers, cannot escape the charge of internal dissension even though he may die for Christ's name. For it is written: *He who hates his brother is a murderer*, nor can he attain the kingdom of heaven. God cannot abide a murderer. He cannot be united with Christ, who has preferred to imitate Judas rather than Christ.

Prayer should be expressed in deeds as well as words

Dear friends, why does the fact that God has taught us such a prayer as this astonish us? Did he not express all of our prayers in his own words of life? Indeed, this was already foretold by Isaiah. Filled with the Holy Spirit, he spoke of the majesty and fidelity of God: *The Lord will speak a final brief word of justice, a word throughout the world.* Our Lord, Jesus Christ, came for all mankind. He gathered together male and female, the learned and the unlearned, the old and the young and taught them his saving doctrine. He did not want his disciples to be burdened by memorizing his teaching; he made a complete summary of his commands such as was necessary for a trusting faith, and could be quickly learned.

Thus, he summarized his teaching on the mystery of eternal life and its meaning with an admirable, divine brevity: *And eternal life is this: to know you, the only true God, and Jesus Christ whom you sent.* Again, in quoting the first and the greatest precept of the law and the prophets, he spoke in the same way: *Listen, Israel, the Lord your God is one Lord, and: you shall love the Lord your God with all your heart, with all your soul, and with all your strength. This is the first commandment. The second is like it: You must love your neighbor as yourself. On these two commandments depends all that is contained in the law and the prophets.* On another occasion, the Lord said: *Always treat others as you would like them to treat you: that is the meaning of the law and the prophets.*

God taught us to pray not only by his words, but also by his actions. He taught us by his own example for he often prayed on our behalf. The Scripture says: *He withdrew to the wilderness and prayed.* And again: *He went into the hills to pray and he spent the whole night in prayer to God.*

Was the sinless Lord praying for himself? No, he was praying and interceding on our behalf. He explains this to Peter: *Behold Satan demanded that he might sift you like wheat, but I have prayed for you that your faith may not fail.* Later on, he prayed to the Father for everyone: *I am not praying for these only, but also for those who will believe in me through their preaching, that they may be one; just as you, Father, are in me, and I in you, that they also may be one in us.* God loves us; for the sake of our salvation, he is generous toward us. He is not satisfied with redeeming us by his blood. He also prays to the Father on our behalf. Consider the love exemplified in that prayer. The Father and Son are one; we too are to abide in that oneness.

CHAPTER IV

THE LORD'S PRAYER
"OUR FATHER!"
Catechism of the Catholic Church

2759

esus "was praying at a certain place, and when he ceased, one of his disciples said to him 'Lord, teach us to pray, as John taught his disciples.'"[1] In response to this request the Lord entrusts to his disciples and to his Church the fundamental Christian prayer. St. Luke presents a brief text of five petitions,[2] while St. Matthew gives a more developed version of seven petitions.[3] The liturgical tradition of the Church has retained St. Matthew's text:

> Our Father who art in heaven,
> hallowed be thy name.
> Thy kingdom come.
> Thy will be done on earth, as it is in heaven.
> Give us this day our daily bread,
> and forgive us our trespasses,
> as we forgive those who trespass against us,
> and lead us not into temptation,
> but deliver us from evil.

2760   Very early on, liturgical usage concluded the Lord's Prayer with a doxology. In the *Didache*, we find," For yours are the power and the glory for ever."[4] The *Apostolic Constitutions* add to the beginning: "the kingdom," and this is the formula retained to our day in ecumenical prayer.[5] The Byzantine tradition adds after "the glory" the words "Father, Son, and Holy Spirit." The *Roman Missal* develops the last petition in the explicit perspective of "awaiting our blessed hope" and of the Second Coming of our Lord Jesus Christ.[6] Then comes the assembly's acclamation or the repetition of the doxology from the Apostolic Constitutions.

Article 1

"THE SUMMARY OF THE WHOLE GOSPEL"

2761 The Lord's Prayer " is truly the summary of the whole gospel."[7] "Since the Lord... after handing over the practice of prayer, said elsewhere, 'Ask and you will receive,' and since everyone has petitions which are peculiar to his circumstances, the regular and appropriate prayer {the Lord's Prayer} is said first, as the foundation of further desires."[8]

I. At the Center of the Scriptures

2762 After showing how the psalms are the principal food of Christian prayer and flow together in the petitions of the Our Father, St. Augustine concludes:

> Run through all the words of the holy prayers {in Scripture}, and I do not think that you will find anything in them that is not contained and included in the Lord's Prayer.[9]

2763 All the Scriptures – the Law, the Prophets, and the Psalms – are fulfilled in Christ[10]. The Gospel is this "Good News." Its first proclamation is summarized by St. Matthew in the Sermon on the Mount[11]; the prayer to our Father is at the center of this proclamation. It is in this context that each petition bequeathed to us by the Lord is illuminated:

> The Lord's Prayer is the most perfect of prayers.... In it we ask, not only for all the things we can rightly desire, but also in the sequence that they should be desired. This prayer not only teaches us to ask for things, but also in what order we should desire them[12].

2764 The Sermon on the Mount is teaching for life, the Our Father is a prayer; but in both the one and the other the Spirit of the Lord gives new form to our desires, those inner movements that animate our lives. Jesus teaches us this new life by his words; he teaches us to ask for it by our prayer. The rightness of our life in him will depend on the rightness of our prayer.

II. "The Lord's Prayer"

2765   The traditional expression "the Lord's Prayer" — *oratio Dominica* — means that the prayer to our Father is taught and given to us by the Lord Jesus. The prayer that comes to us from Jesus is truly unique: it is "of the Lord." On the one hand, in the words of this prayer the only Son gives us the words the Father gave him[13]: he is the master of our prayer. On the other, as Word incarnate, he knows in his human heart the needs of his human brothers and sisters and reveals them to us: he is the model of our prayer.

2766   But Jesus does not give us a formula to repeat mechanically.[14] As in every vocal prayer, it is through the Word of God that the Holy Spirit teaches the children of God to pray to their Father. Jesus not only gives us the words of our filial prayer; at the same time he gives us the Spirit by whom these words become in us "spirit and life."[15] Even more, the proof and possibility of our filial prayer is that the Father "sent the Spirit of his Son into our hearts, crying, 'Abba! Father!'"[16] Since our prayer sets forth our desires before God, it is again the Father, "he who searches the hearts of men," who "knows what is the mind of the Spirit, because the Spirit intercedes for the saints according to the will of God."[17] The prayer to Our Father is inserted into the mysterious mission of the Son and of the Spirit.

III. The Prayer of the Church

2767   This indivisible gift of the Lord's words and of the Holy Spirit who gives life to them in the hearts of believers has been received and lived by the Church from the beginning. The first communities prayed the Lord's Prayer three times a day,[18] in place of the "Eighteen Benedictions" customary in Jewish piety.

2768   According to the apostolic tradition, the Lord's Prayer is essentially rooted in liturgical prayer:

> [The Lord] teaches us to make prayer in common for all our brethren. For he did not say "my Father" who art in heaven, but "our" Father, offering petitions for the common Body.[19]

In all the liturgical traditions, the Lord's Prayer is an integral part of the major hours of the Divine Office. In the three sacraments of

Christian initiation its ecclesial character is especially in evidence.

2769 In Baptism and Confirmation, the handing on (*traditio*) of the Lord's Prayer signifies new birth into the divine life. Since Christian prayer is our speaking to God with the very word of God, those who are "born anew... through the living and abiding word of God"[20] learn to invoke their Father by the one Word he always hears. They can henceforth do so, for the seal of the Holy Spirit's anointing is indelibly placed on their hearts, ears, lips, indeed their whole filial being. This is why most of the patristic commentaries on the Our Father are addressed to catechumens and neophytes. When the church prays the Lord's Prayer, it is always the people made up of the "new-born" who pray and obtain mercy.[21]

2770 In the *Eucharistic liturgy*, the Lord's Prayer appears as the prayer of the whole Church and there reveals its full meaning and efficacy. Placed between the *anaphora* (the Eucharistic prayer) and the communion, the Lord's Prayer sums up on the one hand all the petitions and intercessions expressed in the movement of the *epiclesis* and, on the other, knocks at the door of the Banquet of the kingdom which sacramental communion anticipates.

2771 In the Eucharist, the Lord's Prayer also reveals the *eschatological* character of its petitions. It is the proper prayer of "the end-time," the time of salvation that began with the outpouring of the Holy Spirit and will be fulfilled with the Lord's return. The petitions addressed to our Father, as distinct from the prayers of the old covenant, rely on the mystery of salvation already accomplished, once for all, in Christ crucified and risen.

2772 From this unshakable faith springs forth the hope that sustains each of the seven petitions, which express the groanings of the present age, this time of patience and expectation during which "it does not yet appear what we shall be."[22] The Eucharist and the Lord's Prayer look eagerly for the Lord's return, "until he comes."[23]

In Brief

2773 In response to his disciples' request "Lord, teach us to pray"

(*Lk* 11:1), Jesus entrusts them with the fundamental Christian prayer, the Our Father.

2774 "The Lord's Prayer is truly the summary of the whole gospel,"[24] the "most perfect of prayers."[25] It is at the center of the Scriptures.

2775 It is called "the Lord's Prayer" because it comes to us from the Lord Jesus, the master and model of our prayer.

2776 The Lord's Prayer is the quintessential prayer of the Church. It is an integral part of the major hours of the Divine Office and of the sacraments of Christian initiation: Baptism, Confirmation, and Eucharist. Integrated into the Eucharist it reveals the escatological character of its petitions, hoping for the Lord, "until he comes" (*1 Cor* 11:26).

Article 2
"OUR FATHER WHO ART IN HEAVEN"

I. "We Dare To Say"
2777 In the Roman liturgy, the Eucharistic assembly is invited to pray to our heavenly Father with filial boldness; the Eastern liturgies develop and use similar expressions: "dare in all confidence," "make us worthy of…." From the burning bush Moses heard a voice saying to him, "Do not come near; put off your shoes from your feet, for the place on which you are standing is holy ground."[26] Only Jesus could cross that threshold of the divine holiness, for "when he had made purification for sins," he brought us into the Father's presence: "Here am I, and the children God has given me."[27]

> Our awareness of our status as slaves would make us sink into the ground and our earthly condition would dissolve into dust, if the authority of our Father himself and the Spirit of his Son had not impelled us to this cry… 'Abba, Father!'… When would a mortal dare call God 'Father,' if man's innermost being were not animated by power from on high?"[28]

2778 This power of the Spirit who introduces us to the Lord's Prayer is expressed in the liturgies of East and of West by the beautiful, characteristically Christian expression: *parrhesia*, straightforward simplicity, filial trust, joyous assurance, humble boldness, the certainty of being loved.[29]

II. "Father!"

2779   Before we make our own this first exclamation of the Lord's Prayer, we must humbly cleanse our hearts of certain false images drawn "from this world." *Humility* makes us recognize that "no one knows the Son except the Father, and no one know the Father except the Son and anyone to whom the Son chooses to reveal him," that is, "to little children."[30] The *purification* of our hearts has to do with paternal or maternal images, stemming from our personal and cultural history, and influencing our relationship with God. God our Father transcends the categories of the created world. To impose our own ideas in this area "upon him" would be to fabricate idols to adore or pull down. To pray to the Father is to enter into his mystery as he is and as the Son has revealed him to us.

The expression God the Father had never been revealed to anyone. When Moses himself asked God who he was, he heard another name. The Father's name has been revealed to us in the Son, for the name "Son" implies the new name "Father."[31]

2780   We can invoke God as "Father" because *he is revealed to us* by his Son become man and because his Spirit makes him known to us. The personal relation of the Son to the Father is something that man cannot conceive of nor the angelic powers even dimly see: and yet, the Spirit of the Son grants a participation in that very relation to us who believe that Jesus is the Christ and that we are born of God.[32]

2781   When we pray to the Father, we are *in communion with him* and with his Son, Jesus Christ.[33] Then we know and recognize him with an ever new sense of wonder. The first phrase of the Our Father is a blessing of adoration before it is a supplication. For it is the glory of God that we should recognize him as "Father," the true God. We give him thanks for having revealed his name to us, for the gift of believing in it, and for the indwelling of his Presence in us.

2782 We can adore the Father because he has caused us to be reborn to his life by *adopting* us as his children in his only Son: by Baptism, he incorporates us into the Body of his Christ; through the anointing of his Spirit who flows from the head to the members, he makes us other "Christs."

> God, indeed, who has predestined us to adoption as his sons, has conformed us to the glorious Body of Christ. So then you who have become sharers in Christ are appropriately called "Christs."[34]

> The new man, reborn and restored to his God by grace, says first of all, "Father!" because he has now begun to be a son.[35]

2783 Thus, the Lord's Prayer *reveals us to ourselves* at the same time that it reveals the Father to us.[36]

> O man, you did not dare to raise your face to heaven, you lowered your eyes to the earth, and suddenly you have received the grace of Christ: all your sins have been forgiven. From being a wicked servant you have become a good son.....Then raise your eyes to the Father who has begotten you through Baptism, to the Father who has redeemed you through his Son, and say: "Our Father....." But do not claim any privilege. He is Father of us all, because while he has begotten only Christ, he has created us. Then also say by his grace, "Our Father," so that you may merit being his son.[37]

2784 The free gift of adoption requires on our part continual conversion and *new life*. Praying to our Father should develop in us two fundamental dispositions:

First, *the desire to become like him*: though created in his image, we are restored to his likeness by grace; and we must respond to this grace.

> We must remember... and know that when we call

God "our Father" we ought to behave as sons of God.³⁸

You cannot call the God of all kindness your Father if you preserve a cruel and inhuman heart; for in this case you no longer have in you the marks of the heavenly Father's kindness.³⁹

We must contemplate the beauty of the Father without ceasing and adorn our own souls accordingly.⁴⁰

2785 Second, *a humble and trusting heart* that enables us "to turn and become like children⁴¹ for it is to "little children" that the Father is revealed.⁴²

[The prayer is accomplished] by the contemplation of God alone, and by the warmth of love, through which the soul, molded and directed to love him, speaks very familiarly to God as to its own Father with special devotion.⁴³

Our Father: at this name love is aroused in us... and the confidence of obtaining what we are about to ask.... What would he not give to his children who ask, since he has already granted them the gift of being his children?⁴⁴

III. "Our" Father

2786 "Our" Father refers to God. The adjective, as used by us, does not express possession, but an entirely new relationship with God.

2787 When we say "our" Father, we recognize first that all his promises of love announced by the prophets are fulfilled in the *new and eternal covenant* in his Christ: we have become "his" people and he is henceforth "our" God. This new relationship is the purely gratuitous gift of belonging to each other; we are to respond to "grace and truth" given us in Jesus Christ with love and faithfulness.⁴⁵

2788 Since the Lord's Prayer is that of his people in the "end-time," this "our" also expresses the certitude of our hope in God's ultimate promise: in the new Jerusalem he will say to the victor, "I will be his God and he shall be my son."[46]

2789　When we pray to "our" Father, we personally address the Father of our Lord Jesus Christ. By doing so we do not divide the Godhead, since the Father is its "source and origin," but rather confess that the Son is eternally begotten by him and the Holy Spirit proceeds from him. We are not confusing the persons, for we confess that our communion is with the Father and his Son, Jesus Christ, in their one Holy Spirit. The *Holy Trinity* is consubstantial and indivisible. When we pray to the Father, we adore and glorify him together with the Son and the Holy Spirit.

2790　Grammatically, "our" qualifies a reality common to more than one person. There is only one God, and he is recognized as Father by those who, through faith in his only Son, are reborn of him by water and the Spirit.[47] The *Church* is this new communion of God and men. United with the only Son, who has become "the firstborn among many brethren," she is in communion with one and the same Father in one and the same Holy Spirit.[48] In praying "our" Father, each of the baptized is praying in this communion: "The company of those who believed were of one heart and soul."[49]

2791　For this reason, in spite of the divisions among Christians, this prayer to "our" Father remains our common patrimony and an urgent summons for all the baptized. In communion by faith in Christ and by Baptism, they ought to join in Jesus' prayer for the unity of his disciples.[50]

2792　Finally, if we pray the Our Father sincerely, we leave individualism behind, because the love that we receive frees us from it. The "our" at the beginning of the Lord's Prayer, like the "us" of the last four petitions, excludes no one. If we are to say it truthfully, our divisions and oppositions have to be overcome.[51]

2793　The baptized cannot pray to "our" Father without bringing before him all those for whom he gave his beloved Son. God's love has no bounds, neither should our prayer.[52] Praying "our" Father opens to us the dimensions of his love revealed in Christ: praying with and for all who do not yet know him, so that Christ may "gather into one the children of God."[53] God's care for all men and for the whole of creation has inspired all the great practitioners of prayer; it should extend our prayer to the full breadth of love whenever we dare to say "our" Father.

IV. "Who Art In Heaven"

2794   This biblical expression does not mean a place ("space"), but a way of being; it does not mean that God is distant, but majestic. Our Father is not "elsewhere": he transcends everything we can conceive of his holiness. It is precisely because he is thrice-holy that he is so close to the humble and contrite heart.

> "Our Father who art in heaven" is rightly understood to mean that God is in the hearts of the just, as in his holy temple. At the same time, it means that those who pray should desire the one they invoke to dwell in them.[54]

> "Heaven" could also be those who bear the image of the heavenly world, and in whom God dwells and tarries.[55]

2795   The symbol of the heavens refers us back to the mystery of the covenant we are living when we pray to our Father. He is in heaven, his dwelling place; the Father's house is our homeland. Sin has exiled us from the land of the covenant,[56] but conversion of heart enables us to return to the Father, to heaven.[57] In Christ, then, heaven and earth are reconciled,[58] for the Son alone "descended from heaven" and causes us to ascend there with him, by his Cross, Resurrection, and Ascension.[59]

2796   When the Church prays "our Father who art in heaven," she is professing that we are the People of God, already seated "with him in the heavenly places in Christ Jesus" and "hidden with Christ in God;"[60] yet at the same time, "here indeed we groan, and long to put on our heavenly dwelling."[61]

[Christians] are in the flesh, but do not live according to the flesh. They spend their lives on earth, but are citizens of heaven.[62]

In Brief

2797   Simple and faithful trust, humble and joyous assurance are the proper dispositions for one who prays the Our Father.

2798   We can invoke God as "Father" because the Son of God made man has revealed him to us. In this Son, through Baptism, we are incorporated and adopted as sons of God.

2799   The Lord's Prayer brings us into communion with the Father and with his Son, Jesus Christ. At the same time, it reveals us to ourselves (cf. GS 22:1).

2800   Praying to our Father should develop in us the will to become like him and foster in us a humble and trusting heart.

2801   When we say "Our" Father, we are invoking the new covenant in Jesus Christ, communion with the Holy Trinity, and the divine love which spreads through the Church to encompass the world.

2802   "Who art in heaven" does not refer to a place but to God's majesty and his presence in the hearts of the just. Heaven, the Father's house, is the true homeland toward which we are heading and to which, already, we belong.

Article 3
THE SEVEN PETITIONS

2803   After we have placed ourselves in the presence of God our Father to adore and to love and to bless him, the Spirit of adoption stirs up in our hearts seven petitions, seven blessings. The first three, more theological, draw us toward the glory of the Father; the last four, as ways toward him, commend our wretchedness to his grace. "Deep calls to deep."[63]

2804   The first series of petitions carries us toward him, for his own sake: *thy* name, *thy* kingdom, *thy* will! It is characteristic of love to think first of the one whom we love. In none of the three petitions do we mention ourselves; the burning desire, even anguish, of the beloved Son for his Father's glory seizes us:[64] "hallowed be thy name, thy kingdom come, thy will be done....." These three supplications were already answered in the saving sacrifice of Christ, but they are hence forth directed in hope toward their final fulfillment, for God is not yet all in all.[65]

2805   The second series of petitions unfolds with the same movement as certain Eucharistic epicleses: as an offering up of our expectations, that draws down upon itself the eyes of the Father of mercies. They go up from us and concern us from this very moment, in our present world: "give *us*... forgive *us*... lead *us* not... deliver *us*....." The fourth and fifth petitions concern our life as such – to be fed and to be healed of sin; the last two concern our battle for the victory of life – that battle of prayer.

2806   By the three first petitions, we are strengthened in faith, filled with hope, and set aflame by charity. Being creatures and still sinners, we have to petition for us, for that "us" bound by the world and history, which we offer to the boundless love of God. For through the name of his Christ and the reign of his Holy Spirit, our Father accomplishes his plan of salvation, for us and for the whole world.

I. "HALLOWED BE THY NAME"

2807   The term" to hallow" is to be understood here not primarily in its causative sense (only God hallows, makes holy), but above all in an evaluative sense: to recognize as holy, to create in a holy way. And so, in adoration, this invocation is sometimes understood as praise and thanksgiving.[66] But this petition is here taught to us by Jesus as an optative: a petition, a desire, and an expectation in which God and man are involved. Beginning with this first petition to our Father, we are immersed in the innermost mystery of his Godhead and the drama of the salvation of our humanity. Asking the Father that his name be made holy draws us into his plan of loving kindness for the fullness of time, "according to his purpose which he set forth in Christ," that we might "be holy and blameless before him in love."[67]

2808 In the decisive moments of his economy, God reveals his name, but he does so by accomplishing his work. This work, then, is realized for us and in us only if his name is hallowed by us and in us.

2809 The holiness of God is the inaccessible center of his eternal mystery. What is revealed of it in creation and history, Scripture calls "glory," the radiance of his majesty.[68] In making man in his image and likeness, God "crowned him with glory and honor," but by sinning, man fell "short of the glory of God."[69] From that time on, God was to manifest his holiness by revealing and giving his name, in order to restore man to the image of his Creator.[70]

2810 In the promise to Abraham and the oath that accompanied it,[71] God commits himself but without disclosing his name. He begins to reveal it to Moses and makes it known clearly before the eyes of the whole people when he saves them from the Egyptians: "he has triumphed gloriously."[72] From the covenant of Sinai onwards, this people is "his own" and it is to be a "holy (or "consecrated": the same word is used for both in Hebrew) nation,"[73] because the name of God dwells in it.

2811 In spite of the holy Law that again and again their Holy God gives them — "you shall be holy, for I the LORD your God am holy" — and although the Lord shows patience for the sake of his name, the people turn away from the Holy One of Israel and profane his name among the nations.[74] For this reason, the just ones of the old covenant, the poor survivors returned from exile, and the prophets burned with passion for the name.

2812 Finally, in Jesus the name of the Holy God is revealed and given to us, in the flesh, as Savior, revealed by what he is, by his word, and by his sacrifice.[75] This is the heart of his priestly prayer: "Holy Father... for their sake I consecrate myself, that they also may be consecrated in truth."[76] Because he "sanctifies" his own name, Jesus reveals to us the name of the Father.[77] At the end of Christ's Passover, the Father gives him the name that is above all names: "Jesus Christ is Lord, to the glory of God the Father."[78]

2813 In the waters of Baptism, we have been "washed... sanctified... justified in the name of the Lord Jesus Christ and in the Spirit of our God."[79] Our Father calls us to holiness in the whole of our life, and since "he is the source of [our] life in Christ Jesus, who became for us wisdom from God, and... sanctification,"[80] both his glory and our life depend on the hallowing of his name in us and by us. Such is the urgency of our first petition.

> By whom is God hallowed, since he is the one who hallows? But since he said, "you shall be holy to me; for I the LORD am holy," we seek and ask that we who were sanctified in Baptism may persevere in what we have begun to be. And we ask this daily, for we need sanctification daily, so that we who fail daily may cleanse away our sins by being sanctified continually.... We pray that this sanctification may remain in us.[81]

2814 The sanctification of his name among the nations depends inseparably on our *life* and our *prayer*:

> We ask God to hallow his name, which by its own holiness saves and makes holy all creation.... It is this name that gives salvation to a lost world. But we ask that this name of God should be hallowed in us through our actions. For God's name is blessed when we live well, but is blasphemed when we live wickedly. As the Apostle says: "The name of God is blasphemed among the Gentiles because of you." We ask then that, just as the name of God is holy, so we may obtain his holiness in our souls.[82]

> When we say "hallowed be thy name," we ask that it should be hallowed in us, who are in him; but also in others whom God's grace still awaits, that we may obey the precept that obligates us to pray for everyone, even our enemies. That is why we do not say expressly "hallowed be thy name 'in us,'" for we ask that it be

so in all men.[83]

2815 This petition embodies all the others. Like the six petitions that follow, it is fulfilled by *the prayer of Christ*. Prayer to our Father is our prayer, if it is prayed *in the name* of Jesus.[84] In his priestly prayer, Jesus asks: "Holy Father, protect in your name those whom you have given me."[85]

II. "THY KINGDOM COME"

2816 In the New Testament, the word *basileia* can be translated by "kingship" (abstract noun), "kingdom" (concrete noun) or "reign" (action noun). The Kingdom of God lies ahead of us. It is brought near in the Word incarnate, it is proclaimed throughout the whole Gospel, and it has come in Christ's death and Resurrection. The Kingdom of God has been coming since the Last Supper and, in the Eucharist, it is in our midst. The kingdom will come in glory when Christ hands it over to his Father:

> It may even be... that the Kingdom of God means Christ himself, whom we daily desire to come, and whose coming we wish to be manifested quickly to us. For as he is our resurrection, since in him we rise, so he can also be understood as the Kingdom of God, for in him we shall reign.[86]

2817 This petition is "*Marana tha*," the cry of the Spirit and the Bride: "Come, Lord Jesus."

> Even if it had not been prescribed to pray for the coming of the kingdom, we would willingly have brought forth this speech, eager to embrace our hope. In indignation the souls of the martyrs under the altar cry out to the Lord: "O Sovereign Lord, holy and true, how long before you judge and avenge our blood on those who dwell upon the earth?" For their retribution is ordained for the end of the world. Indeed, as soon as possible, Lord, may your kingdom come!"[87]

2818 In the Lord's Prayer, "thy kingdom come" refers primarily to the final coming of the reign of God through Christ's return.[88] But, far from distracting the Church from her mission in this present world, this desire commits her to it all the more strongly. Since Pentecost, the coming of that Reign is the work of the Spirit of the Lord who "complete[s] his work on earth and brings us the fullness of grace."[89]

2819 "The kingdom of God [is] righteousness and peace and joy in the Holy Spirit."[90] The end-time in which we live is the age of the outpouring of the Spirit. Ever since Pentecost, a decisive battle has been joined between "the flesh" and the Spirit.[91]

> Only a pure soul can boldly say: "Thy kingdom come." One who has heard Paul say, "Let not sin therefore reign in your moral bodies," and has purified himself in action, thought, and word will say to God: "Thy kingdom come!"[92]

2820 By a discernment according to the Spirit, Christians have to distinguish between the growth of the Reign of God and the progress of the culture and society in which they are involved. This distinction is not a separation. Man's vocation to eternal life does not suppress, but actually reinforces, his duty to put into action in this world the energies and means received from the Creator to serve justice and peace.[93]

2821 This petition is taken up and granted in the prayer *of* Jesus which is present and effective in the Eucharist; it bears its fruit in new life in keeping with the Beatitudes.[94]

III. "THY WILL BE DONE ON EARTH AS IT IS IN HEAVEN"

2822 Our Father "desires all men to be saved and to come to the knowledge of the truth."[95] He "is forbearing toward you, not wishing that any should perish."[96] His commandment is "that you love one another; even as I have loved you, that you also love one another."[97] This commandment summarizes all the others and expresses his entire will.

2823 "He has made known to us the mystery of his will, according to his good pleasure that he set forth in Christ... to gather up all things in him, things in heaven and things on earth. In Christ we have also obtained an inheritance, having been destined according to the purpose of him who accomplishes all things according to his counsel and will."[98] We ask insistently for this loving plan to be fully realized on earth as it is already in heaven.

2824 In Christ, and through his human will, the will of the Father has been perfectly fulfilled once for all. Jesus said on entering into this world: "Lo, I have come to do your will, O God."[99] Only Jesus can say: "I always do what is pleasing to him."[100] In the prayer of his agony, he consents totally to this will: "not my will, but yours be done."[101] For this reason, Jesus "gave himself for our sins to deliver us from the present evil age, according to the will of our God and Father."[102] "And by that will we have been sanctified through the offering of the body of Jesus Christ once for all."[103]

2825 "Although he was a Son, [Jesus] learned obedience through what he suffered."[104] How much more reason have we sinful creatures to learn obedience – we who in him have become children of adoption. We ask our Father to unite our will to his Son's, in order to fulfill his will, his plan of salvation for the life of the world. We are radically incapable of this, but united with Jesus and with the power of his Holy Spirit, we can surrender our will to him and decide to choose what his Son has always chosen: to do what is pleasing to the Father.[105]

> In committing ourselves to [Christ], we can become one spirit with him, and thereby accomplish his will, in such a way that it will be perfect on earth as it is in heaven.[106]

> Consider how [Jesus Christ] teaches us to be humble, by making us see that our virtue does not depend on our work alone but on grace from on

high. He commands each of the faithful who prays to do so universally, for the whole world. For he did not say "thy will be done in me or in us," but "on earth," the whole earth, so that error may be banished from it, truth take root in it, all vice be destroyed on it, virtue flourish on it, and earth no longer differ from heaven.[107]

2826 By prayer we can discern "what is the will of God" and obtain the endurance to do it.[108] Jesus teaches us that one enters the kingdom of heaven not by speaking words, but by doing "the will of my Father in heaven."[109]

2827 "If any one is a worshiper of God and does his will, God listens to him."[110] Such is the power of the Church's prayer in the name of her Lord, above all in the Eucharist. Her prayer is also a communion of intercession with the all-holy Mother of God[111] and all the saints who have been pleasing to the Lord because they willed his will alone:

> It would not be inconsistent with the truth to understand the words, "Thy will be done on earth as it is in heaven," to mean: "in the Church as in our Lord Jesus Christ himself"; or "in the Bride who has been betrothed, just as in the Bridegroom who has accomplished the will of the Father."[112]

IV. "GIVE US THIS DAY OUR DAILY BREAD"

2828 "Give us": The trust of children who look to their Father for everything is beautiful. "He makes his sun rise on the evil and on the good, and sends rain on the just and on the unjust."[113] He gives to all the living "their food in due season."[1114] Jesus teaches us this petition, because it glorifies our Father by acknowledging how good he is, beyond all goodness.

2829 "Give us" also expresses the covenant. We are his and he is ours, for our sake. But this "us" also recognizes him as the Father of all men and we pray to him for them all, in solidarity with their needs and sufferings.

2830 *"Our bread"*: The Father who gives us life cannot not but give us the nourishment life requires – all appropriate goods and blessings, both material and spiritual. In the Sermon on the Mount, Jesus insists on the filial trust that cooperates with our Father's providence.[115] He is not inviting us to idleness,[116] but wants to relieve us from nagging worry and preoccupation. Such is the filial surrender of the children of God:

> To those who seek the kingdom of God and his righteousness, he has promised to give all else besides. Since everything indeed belongs to God, he who possesses God wants for nothing, if he himself is not found wanting before God.[117]

2831 But the presence of those who hunger because they lack bread opens up another profound meaning of this petition. The drama of hunger in the world calls Christians who pray sincerely to exercise responsibility toward their brethren, both in their personal behavior and in their solidarity with the human family. This petition of the Lord's Prayer cannot be isolated from the parables of the poor man Lazarus and of the Last Judgment.[118]

2832 As leaven in the dough, the newness of the kingdom should make the earth "rise" by the Spirit of Christ.[119] This must be shown by the establishment of justice in personal and social, economic and international relations, without ever forgetting that there are no just structures without people who want to be just.

2833 "Our" bread is the "one" loaf for the "many." In the beatitudes "poverty" is the virtue of sharing: it calls us to communicate and share both material and spiritual goods, not by coercion but out of love, so that the abundance of some may remedy the needs of others.[120]

2834 "Pray and work."[121] "Pray as if everything depended on God and work as if everything depended on you."[122] Even when we have done our work, the food we receive is still a gift from our Father; it is good to ask him for it with thanksgiving, as Christian families do when saying grace at meals.

2835 This petition, with the responsibility it involves, also applies to another hunger from which men are perishing: "Man does not live by bread alone, but... by every word that proceeds from the mouth of God,"[123] that is, by the Word he speaks and the Spirit he breathes forth. Christians must make every effort "to proclaim the good news to the poor." There is a famine on earth, "not a famine of bread, nor a thirst for water, but of hearing the words of the LORD."[124] For this reason, the specifically Christian sense of this fourth petition concerns the Bread of Life: The Word of God accepted in faith, the Body of Christ received in the Eucharist.[125]

2836 "*This day*" is also an expression of trust taught us by the Lord,[126] which we would never have presumed to invent. Since it refers above all to his Word and to the Body of his Son, this "today" is not only that of our mortal time, but also the "today" of God.

> If you receive the bread each day, each day is today for you. If Christ is yours today, he rises for you every day. How can this be? "You are my Son, today I have begotten you." Therefore, "today" is when Christ rises.[127]

2837 "*Daily*" (*epiousios*) occurs nowhere else in the New Testament. Taken in a temporal sense, this word is a pedagogical repetition of "this day,"[128] to confirm us in trust "without reservation." Taken in the qualitative sense, it signifies what is necessary for life, and more broadly every good thing sufficient for subsistence.[129] Taken literally (*epi-ousios*: "super-essential"), it refers directly to the Bread of Life, the Body of Christ, the "medicine of immortality," without which we have no life within us.[130] Finally, in this connection, its heavenly meaning is evident: "this day" is the Day of the Lord, the day of the feast of the kingdom, anticipated in the Eucharist that is already the foretaste of the kingdom to come. For this reason it is fitting for the Eucharistic liturgy to be celebrated each day.

> The Eucharist is our daily bread. The power belonging to this divine food makes it a bond of union. Its effect is then understood as unity, so that, gathered into his Body and made members of him, we may become what we receive.... This also is our daily bread: the readings you hear each day in church and the hymns you hear and sing. All these are necessities for our pilgrimage.[131]

> The Father in heaven urges us, as children of heaven, to ask for the bread of heaven. [Christ] himself is the bread who, sown in the Virgin, raised up in the flesh, kneaded in the Passion, baked in the oven of the tomb, reserved in churches, brought to altars, furnishes the faithful each day with food from heaven.[132]

V. "AND FORGIVE US OUR TRESPASSES, AS WE FORGIVE THOSE WHO TRESPASS AGAINST US"

2838 This petition is astonishing. If it consisted only of the first phrase, "And forgive us our trespasses," it might have been included, implicitly, in the first three petitions of the Lord's Prayer, since Christ's sacrifice is "that sins may be forgiven." But, according to the second phrase, our petition will not be heard unless we have first met a strict requirement. Our petition looks to the future, but our response must come first, for the two parts are joined by the single word "as."

And forgive us our trespasses...

2839 With bold confidence, we began praying to our Father. In begging him that his name be hallowed, we were in fact asking him that we ourselves might be always made more holy. But though we are clothed with the baptismal garment, we do not cease to sin, to turn away from God. Now, in this new petition, we return to him like the prodigal son and, like the tax collector, recognize that we are sinners before him.[133] Our petition begins with a "confession" of our wretchedness and his mercy. Our hope is firm because, in his Son, "we have redemption, the forgiveness of sins."[134] We find the efficacious and undoubted sign of his forgiveness in the sacraments of his Church.[135]

2840 Now – and this is daunting – this outpouring of mercy cannot penetrate our hearts as long as we have not forgiven those who have trespassed against us. Love, like the Body of Christ, is indivisible; we cannot love the God we cannot see if we do not love the brother or sister we do see.[136] In refusing to forgive our brothers and sisters, our hearts are closed and their hardness makes them impervious to the Father's merciful love; but in confessing our sins, our hearts are opened to his grace.

2841 This petition is so important that it is the only one to which the Lord returns and which he develops explicitly in the Sermon on the Mount.[137] This crucial requirement of the covenant mystery is possible for man. But "with God all things are possible."[138]

...as we forgive those who trespass against us

2842 This "as" is not unique in Jesus' teaching: "You, therefore, must be perfect, *as* your heavenly Father is perfect"; "Be merciful, even *as* your Father is merciful"; "A new commandment I give to you, that you love one another, even *as* I have loved you, that you also love one another."[139] It is impossible to keep the Lord's commandment by imitating the divine model from outside; there has to be a vital participation, coming from the depths of the heart, in the holiness and the mercy and the love of our God. Only the Spirit by whom we live can make "ours" the same mind that was in Christ Jesus.[140] Then the unity of forgiveness becomes possible and we find ourselves "forgiving one another, *as* God in Christ forgave" us.[141]

2843 Thus, the Lord's words on forgiveness, the love that loves to the end,[142] become a living reality. The parable of the merciless servant, which crowns the Lord's teaching on ecclesial communion, ends with these words: "So also my heavenly Father will do to every one of you, if you do not forgive your brother from your heart."[143] It is there, in fact, "in the depths of the *heart*," that everything is bound and loosed. It is not in our power not to feel or to forget an offense; but the heart that offers itself to the Holy Spirit turns injury into compassion and purifies the memory in transforming the hurt into intercession.

2844 Christian prayer extends to the *forgiveness of enemies*,[144] transfiguring the disciple by configuring him to his Master. Forgiveness is a high-point of Christian prayer; only hearts attuned to God's compassion can receive the gift of prayer. Forgiveness also bears witness that, in our world, love is stronger than sin. The martyrs of yesterday and today bear this witness to Jesus. Forgiveness is the fundamental condition of the reconciliation of the children of God with their Father and of men with one another.[145]

2845 There is no limit or measure to this essentially divine forgiveness,[146] whether one speaks of "sins" as in *Luke* (11:4), or "debts" as in *Matthew* (6:12). We are always debtors: "Owe no one anything, except to love one another."[147] The communion of the Holy Trinity is the source and criterion of truth in every relationship. It is lived out in prayer, above all in the Eucharist.[148]

> God does not accept the sacrifice of a sower of disunion, but commands that he depart from the altar so that he may first be reconciled with his brother. For God can be appeased only by prayers that make peace. To God, the better offering is peace, brotherly concord, and a people made one in the unity of the Father, Son, and Holy Spirit.[149]

VI. "AND LEAD US NOT INTO TEMPTATION"

2846 This petition goes to the root of the preceding one, for our sins result from our consenting to temptation; we, therefore, ask our Father not to "lead" us into temptation. It is difficult to translate the Greek verb used by a single English word: the Greek means both "do not allow us to enter into temptation" and "do not let us yield to temptation."[150] "God cannot be tempted by evil and he himself tempts no one";[151] on the contrary, he wants to set us free from evil. We ask him not to allow us to take the way that leads to sin. We are engaged in the battle "between flesh and spirit"; this petition implores the Spirit of discernment and strength.

2847 The Holy Spirit makes us *discern* between trials, which are necessary for the growth of the inner man,[152] and temptation, which leads to sin and death.[153] We must also discern between being tempted and consenting to temptation. Finally, discernment unmasks the lie of temptation, whose object appears to be good, a "delight to the eyes" and desirable,[154] when in reality its fruit is death.

> God does not want to impose the good, but wants free beings.....There is a certain usefulness to temptation. No one but God knows what our soul has received from him, not even we ourselves. But temptation reveals it in order to teach us to know ourselves, and in this way we discover our evil inclinations and are obliged to give thanks for the goods that temptation has revealed to us.[155]

2848 "Lead us not into temptation" implies a *decision of the heart*: "For where your treasure is, there will your heart be also.... No one can serve two masters."[156] "if we live by the Spirit, let us also walk by the Spirit."[157] In this assent to the Holy Spirit, the Father gives us strength. "No testing has overtaken you that is not common to man. God is faithful, and he will not let you be tempted beyond your strength, but with the temptation will also provide the way of escape, so that you may be able to endure it."[158]

2849 Such a battle and such a victory become possible only through prayer. It is by his prayer that Jesus vanquishes the tempter, both at the outset of his public mission and in the ultimate struggle of his agony.[159] In this petition to our heavenly Father, Christ unites us to his battle and his agony. He urges us to *vigilance* of the heart in communion with his own. Vigilance is "custody of the heart," and Jesus prayed for us to the Father" "Keep them in your name."[160] The Holy Spirit constantly seeks to awaken us to keep watch.[161] Finally, this petition takes on all its dramatic meaning in relation to the last temptation of our earthly battle; it asks for *final perseverance*. "Lo, I am coming like a thief! Blessed is he who is awake."[162]

VII. "BUT DELIVER US FROM EVIL"

2850 The last petition to our Father is also included in Jesus' prayer: "I am not asking you to take them out of the world, but I ask you to protect them from the evil one."[163] It touches each of us personally, but it is always "we" who pray, in communion with the whole Church, for the deliverance of the whole human family. The Lord's Prayer continually opens us to the range of God's economy of salvation. Our interdependence in the drama of sin and death is turned into solidarity in the Body of Christ, the "communion of saints."[164]

2851 In this petition, evil is not an abstraction, but refers to a person, Satan, the Evil One, the angel who opposes God. The devil (*dia-bolos*) is the one who "throws himself across" God's plan and his work of salvation accomplished in Christ.

2852 "A murderer from the beginning,... a liar and the father of lies," Satan is "the deceiver of the whole world."[165] Through him sin and death entered the world and by his definitive defeat all creation will be "freed from the corruption of sin and death."[166] Now "we know that anyone born of God does not sin, but He who was born of God keeps him, and the evil one does not touch him. We know that we are of God, and the whole world is in the power of the evil one."[167]

> The Lord who has taken away your sin and pardoned your faults also protects you and keeps you from the wiles of your adversary the devil, so that the enemy, who is accustomed to leading into sin, may not surprise you. One who entrusts himself

to God does not dread the devil. "If God is for us, who is against us?"[168]

2853 Victory over the "prince of this world"[169] was won once for all at the Hour when Jesus freely gave himself up to death to give us his life. This is the judgment of this world, and the prince of this world is "cast out."[170] "He pursued the woman"[171] but had no hold on her: the new Eve, "full of grace" of the Holy Spirit, is preserved from sin and the corruption of death (the Immaculate Conception and the Assumption of the Most Holy Mother of God, Mary, ever virgin). "Then the dragon was angry with the woman, and went off to make war on the rest of her offspring."[172] Therefore, the Spirit and the Church pray: "Come, Lord Jesus,"[173] since his coming will deliver us from the Evil One.

2854 When we ask to be delivered from the Evil One, we pray as well to be freed from all evils, present, past, and future, of which he is the author or instigator. In this final petition, The Church brings before the Father all the distress of the world. Along with deliverance from the evils that overwhelm humanity, she implores the precious gift of peace and the grace of perseverance in expectation of Christ's return. By praying in this way, she anticipates in humility of faith the gathering together of everyone and everything in him who has "the keys of Death and Hades," who "is and who was and who is to come, the Almighty."[174]

> Deliver us, Lord, we beseech you, from every evil and grant us peace in our day, so that aided by your mercy we might be ever free from sin and protected from all anxiety, as we await the blessed hope and the coming of our Savior, Jesus Christ.[175]

ARTICLE 4
THE FINAL DOXOLOGY

2855 The final doxology, "For the kingdom, the power and the glory are yours, now and forever," takes up again, by inclusion, the first three petitions to our Father: the glorification of his name, the coming of his reign, and the power of his saving will. But these prayers are now proclaimed as adoration and thanksgiving, as in the liturgy of heaven.[176] The ruler of this world has mendaciously attributed to himself the three titles of kingship, power, and glory.[177] Christ, the Lord, restores them to his Father and our Father, until he hands over the kingdom to him when the mystery of salvation will be brought to its completion and God will be all in all.[178]

2856 "Then, after the prayer is over you say 'Amen,' which means 'So be it,' thus ratifying with our 'Amen' what is contained in the prayer that God has taught us."[179]

In Brief

2857 In the Our Father, the object of the first three petitions is the glory of the Father: the sanctification of his name, the coming of the kingdom, and the fulfillment of his will. The four others present our wants to him: they ask that our lives be nourished, healed of sin, and made victorious in the struggle of good over evil.

2858 By asking "hallowed be thy name" we enter into God's plan, the sanctification of his name – revealed first to Moses and then in Jesus – by us and in us, in every nation and in each man.

2859 By the second petition, the Church looks first to Christ's return and the final coming of the Reign of God. It also prays for the growth of the Kingdom of God in the "today" of our own lives.

2860 In the third petition, we ask our Father to unite our will to that of his Son, so as to fulfill his plan of salvation in the life of the world.

2861 In the fourth petition, by saying "give us," we express in communion with our brethren our filial trust in our heavenly Father. "Our daily bread" refers to the earthly nourishment necessary to everyone for subsistence, and also to the Bread of Life: the Word of God and the Body of Christ. It is received in God's "today," as the indispensable, (super-) essential nourishment of the feast of the coming Kingdom anticipated in the Eucharist.

2862   The fifth petition begs God's mercy for our offenses, mercy which can penetrate our hearts only if we have learned to forgive our enemies, with the example and help of Christ.

2863   When we say "lead us not into temptation" we are asking God not to allow us to take the path that leads to sin. This petition implores the Spirit of discernment and strength; it requests the grace of vigilance and final perseverance.

2864   In the last petition, "but deliver us from evil," Christians pray to God with the Church to show forth the victory, already won by Christ, over the "ruler of this world,' Satan, the angel personally opposed to God and to his plan of salvation.

2865   By the final "Amen," we express our "fiat" concerning the seven petitions: "So be it."

EPILOGUE
by Fr. Bill McCarthy

ou have journeyed through four treatises on the Our Father. You are no longer the same. You've been urged to trust, and you have trusted. You have been urged to depend upon the Father's mercy, and you have found mercy. You have been urged to become more childlike, so more childlike you are now. You've been asked to receive all good gifts from the Father of mercies, and so you have.

Please take the treasures you have received and spread them to those you meet and love along the way. More than ever, now that you have become a beloved son or daughter, be willing to become a brother and sister to fellow wayfarers along the way. As the very beautiful song, *People Need the Lord*, states so poignantly in its second verse:

"You are called to take His light into a world where wrong seems right.

What could be too great a cost for sharing life with one who's lost.

Through His love your hearts can feel all the pain they bear.

They must hear the words of life only you can share.

People need the Lord, People need the Lord.
At the end of broken dreams, He's the open door."

Hopefully, the Lord in His love and mercy has opened new doors to the Father for you. And hopefully, as you have received, so now shall you give. Now, as you have been taught, so may you teach others to pray, to really pray as Jesus taught us to pray.

APPENDIX A

PRAY LIKE THIS
The Lord's Prayer, *Matthew 6:9-13*

1.   PRAISE
Our Father Who Art In Heaven, Hallowed Be Thy Name

- Various accolades for God
- Various titles of Jesus
- Prayer language (tongues)
- Focus on God instead of self
- Praising God liberates us to rise upwards toward God
- Our problems are nothing compared to God's power
- Read Psalm 145
- Ask the Holy Spirit to help you praise

2. PLAN OF GOD
Thy Kingdom Come, Thy Will Be Done On Earth As It Is In Heaven
- God has a plan
- He wants to reveal it
- Write down the plan as He reveals it to you

3. PROVISION
Give Us This Day Our Daily Bread
- God wants to provide for your needs
- Ask Him
- Accept His decisions as to what is best for you

4. PERSONAL RELATIONSHIPS
Forgive Us Our Trespasses As We Forgive Those Who Trespass Against Us

God says:
- Love one another as I have loved you
- Forgive one another and I will forgive you
- Pray for God to help you to love and to forgive

5. POWER/PROTECTION
Lead Us Not Into Temptation, But Deliver Us From Evil
- God wants to deliver us from ALL evil
- Don't be a fatalistic Christian at the mercy of chance
- Ask God's Spirit to warn you of dangers
- Then abide by the overwhelming feelings He gives you
- Satan attacks our vulnerabilities
- We need not be pawns of our emotions

Ephesians 6:11-18 - *Put on the Armor of Christ*

- *Helmet of Salvation* – Commit your life to Jesus

- *Breastplate of Righteousness* – Confess your sins

- *Belt of Truth* – Live in the light

- *Sword of the Spirit* – Read the Word of God each day

- *Shield of Faith*
  - To withstand the personal darts of Satan
    - Accept the grace of the moment
    - Don't worry about tomorrow

- *Shoes for spreading the Good News*
  - Be an evangelist
    - By example
    - By witnessing as the Spirit leads you

APPENDIX B

LITANY OF PRAISE TO JESUS

Praise You, Jesus, You are my Life, my Love.
Praise You, Jesus, You are the Name above all names.
Praise You, Jesus, You are the King of creation.
Praise You, Jesus, You are the King of the universe.
Praise You, Jesus, You are the Lord of lords.
Praise You, Jesus, You are the Almighty.
Praise You, Jesus, You are Christ, the King.
Praise You, Jesus, You are the Lamb of God.
Praise You, Jesus, You are the Bright Morning Star.
Praise You, Jesus, You are our Champion and Strength.
Praise You, Jesus, You are the Way for our life.
Praise You, Jesus, You are the Only Truth.
Praise You, Jesus, You are the Wonderful Counselor.
Praise You, Jesus, You are the Prince of Peace.
Praise You, Jesus, You are the Light of the World.
Praise You, Jesus, You are the Living Word.
Praise You, Jesus, You are our Redeemer.
Praise You, Jesus, You are the Messiah.
Praise You, Jesus, You are the Anointed One.
Praise You, Jesus, You are the Good Shepherd.
Praise You, Jesus, You are the Lord of hosts.
Praise You, Jesus, You are the Rock of all ages.
Praise You, Jesus, You are the Savior of the World.
Praise You, Jesus, You are the Bread of Life.
Praise You, Jesus, You are the Font of all holiness.
Praise You, Jesus, You are the Living Water.

Praise You, Jesus, You are the True Vine.

Praise You, Jesus, You are my Spouse, my Maker.

Praise You, Jesus, You are our Fortress.

Praise You, Jesus, You are our Deliverer.

Praise You, Jesus, You are our Victory.

Praise You, Jesus, You are our Salvation.

Praise You, Jesus, You are our Wisdom.

Praise You, Jesus, You are our Sanctification.

Praise You, Jesus, You are the great I AM.

Praise You, Jesus, You are the great High Priest.

Praise You, Jesus, You are our Joy.

Praise You, Jesus, You are my Healing and Wholeness.

Praise You, Jesus, You are our Covenant.

Praise You, Jesus, You are the Most High God.

Praise You, Jesus, You are the Just Judge.

Praise You, Jesus, You are my Defense.

Praise You, Jesus, You are my Protector.

Praise You, Jesus, You are my Provider.

Praise You, Jesus, You are the Bridegroom.

Praise You, Jesus, You are my Patience.

Praise You, Jesus, You are the Resurrection and the Life.

Praise You, Jesus, You are the Alpha and the Omega.

Praise You, Jesus, You are all that I need.

Praise You, Jesus, You are all that I want.

Praise You, Jesus, You are worthy of all praise!

THE OUR FATHER
End Notes

CHAPTER II

1 Cf. *Summa Theologica*, II-II, Q.83, art.9.
2 Heb. 4:16.
3 Jas. 1:6.
4 Col.2:3.
5 1 John 2:1.
6 *De Orat. Dom.*
7 Ibid.
8 *Enchiridion* 78; cf. *Summa Theologica*, I-II, Q.74, art. 8, ad 6.
9 *De Fide Orth.*, 3, c.24.
10 Jas. 4:3.
11 Rom. 8:26.
12 Luke 11:1.
13 Augustine, Ep. 130, *ad Probam*.
14 Mt 6:33.
15 Ps. 62:5,6.
16 Mt 6:7.
17 Augustine, Ep. 130, *ad Probam*.
18 Ps. 101:18.
19 Luke 18:10-14.
20 Jth. 9:16.
21 Ps. 31:5,6.
22 Luke 23:43.
23 Luke 18:14.
24 Jas. 5:13.
25 Ps. 108:4.
26 Mark 11:24.
27 Luke 18:1.
28 2 Cor. 12:7-9.
29 Ps. 140:2.
30 Deut. 32:6.
31 Wisd. 14:3.
32 Wisd. 12:18.
33 Rom. 8:17.
34 Rom. 8:15.
35 Mal. 1:6.
36 Ps. 49:23.
37 Isa. 29:13.
38 1 Cor. 6:20.
39 Ps. 98:4.
40 Jer. 3:19.
41 Eph. 5:1,2.
42 Luke 6:36.
43 Mt. 5:48.
44 Heb. 12:9.
45 Exod. 24:7
46 Phil. 2:8
47 2 Kings 6:21,22
48 Prov. 3:11,12
49 1 John 4:20
50 Mal. 2:10
51 Rom. 12:10
52 Heb. 5:9
53 Jas. 1:6
54 Luke 11:13
55 Ps. 122:1
56 Ecclus. 18:23
57 Mt 5:12
58 1 Cor. 15:49
59 Mt 6:21
60 Phil. 3:20
61 Col. 3:1
62 Jer. 14:9
63 Ps. 18:2
64 Eph. 3:17
65 1 John 4:16
66 John 14:23
67 3 Kings 8:27
68 Ps. 101:20
69 Ps. 102:19
70 Ps. 101:13
71 Ps. 101:28
72 Ps. 88:30
73 Aristotle
74 Aristotle, *De Caelo*, 1
75 Jer. 23:24
76 Ps. 102:19
77 Job 36:26
78 Ps. 112:4
79 Isa. 40:18
80 Job 22:14
81 Ps. 18:2
82 Jer. 14:9
83 Ps. 144:18
84 Mt 6:6
85 Job 5:1
86 Jas. 5:16
87 Col. 3:1
88 1 Pet. 1:4
89 1 Cor. 15:48

90 Mark 16:17,18
91 Acts 4:12
92 Phil. 2:10
93 Mt. 16:18; "And the rock was Christ": 1 Cor. 10:4
94 Deut. 4:24
95 Ps. 17:29
96 Augustine, *Confessions* II,10
97 Phil. 3:8
98 Gen. 3:18
99 Gen. 1:2
100 Ps. 135:6
101 Ps. 142:6
102 Rev. 7:14
103 Rev. 1:5
104 Titus 2:12
105 Dan. 7:14.
106 1 Cor. 15:25
107 Ps. 109:1.
108 Amos 5:18.
109 1 Cor. 15:26.
110 Phil. 3:21.
111 1 Tim. 2:4.
112 Mt. 13:41.
113 Isa. 60:21.
114 Rom. 8:21
115 Rev. 5:10.
116 Isa. 28:5.
117 Isa. 64:4.
118 Ps. 102:5.
119 *Summa Theologica*, I-II, Q.69, art.3, ad 3; II-II, Q.89, art. 9, ad 3; Q. 121, art. 2.
120 Isa. 66:14.
121 Isa. 35:10.
122 Augustine, *Confessions* II, 6.
123 Rom. 6:12.
124 Isa. 52:7.
125 *Summa Theologica*, I-II, Q. 69, art. 3, ad 3; II-II, Q. 89, art. 9, ad 3; Q. 121, art 2.
126 Mt. 5:4.
127 Mt. 11:29.
128 Heb. 10:34.
129 Ps. 118:66.
130 Prov. 3:5.
131 Prov. 26:12.
132 Prov. 11:2.
133 John 6:38.
134 Ps. 134.6.
135 Ps. 88:48.
136 John 6:40.
137 Mt. 19:17.
138 Rom. 12:1,2
139 Isa. 48:17
140 Ps 96:11
141 Mt. 5:48.
142 *Super Verb. Ap.*, serm. 15, commenting on John 14:12.
143 Zach. 1:3.
144 1 Cor. 15:10.
145 Rom. 7:23.
146 Gal. 5:17.
147 1 Thess. 4:3.
148 1 Cor. 15:43.
149 Mt. 5:5.
150 Ps. 119:5.
151 2 Cor 5:8.
152 Ps. 125:6,7.
153 Ps. 6:7.
154 Isa. 40:29.
155 Ezech. 2:2.
156 Isa. 11:2.
157 Ecclus. 29:27.
158 1 Tim. 6:8.
159 *Ep. ad Macedon*, 143.
160 Prov. 30:8.
161 Prov. 23:21.
162 Ecclus. 19:1.
163 1 Chr. 29:14.
164 Eccles. 6:1,2.
165 Eccles. 5:12.
166 Job 20:14,15.
167 Mt. 6:31.
168 John 6:51.
169 1 Cor. 11:29.
170 Mt. 4:4.
171 Prov. 20:18.
172 Dan. 4:24.
173 *De Nat. et Grat.*, 36.
174 1 John 1:8.
175 Eph. 4:19.
176 Mt. 18:32.
177 Ps. 31:5.
178 *Summa Theologica Suppl.*, Q.5, art. 2.
179 Jn 20:22,23.
180 *Summa Theologica Suppl.*, Q.25.
181 Ecclus. 28:3.
182 Lk 6:37.
183 Ps. 33:15.
184 Ecclus. 28:2.

185 Isa. 1:16.
186 *Summa Theologica*, I.Q.114, art.2;II-II,Q.97,art.1.
187 Ps. 33:15.
188 Gen. 22.
189 Job 1.
190 Deut. 13:3.
191 Jas. 1:13.
192 Jas. 1:14.
193 Wisd. 9:15.
194 Rom. 7:22,23.
195 Mt. 26:41.
196 Eph. 6:12.
197 1 Thess. 3:5.
198 1 Pet. 5:8.
199 2 Cor. 11:14.
200 Job 40:12.
201 1 Tim. 6:10.
202 Job 37:19.
203 2 Tim. 3:12.
204 Mt. 10:28.
205 Jas. 1:2.
206 Ecclus. 2:1.
207 Jas. 1:12.
208 1 Cor. 10:13.
209 *Summa Theologica*, I-II, Q.70, art. 3.
210 Ps. 70:9.
211 Song of Sol. 8:7.
212 Ethics, III, 1.
213 Ps. 31:8.
214 Ps. 12:4,5.
215 Mt. 5:8
216 2 Tim. 3:12.
217 Rev. 3:8.
218 Job 5:19.
219 Rev. 7:16.
220 2 Cor. 1:8.
221 2 Cor. 7:6.
222 Ps. 93:19.
223 Tob. 3:22.
224 2 Cor. 4:17.
225 Rom. 5:3.
226 Tob. 3:13.
227 Prov. 19:11.
228 Mt. 5:9.
229 *Summa Theologica*, II-II, Q.83, art. 9.
230 Mt. 6:33.
231 Job 35:6,7.

CHAPTER IV
1 Lk 11.
2 Cf. Lk 11:2-4.
3 Cf. Mt 6:9-13.
4 *Didache* 8, 2:Sch 248, 174.
5 *Apostolic Constitutions*, 7, 24, 1:PG 1, 1016.
6 *Titus* 2:13; cf. *Roman Missal* 22, Embolism after the Lord's Prayer.
7 Tertullian, *De orat.* 1: PL 1, 1155
8 Tertullian, *De orat.* 10: PL 1, 1165; cf. *Lk* 11:9.
9 St. Augustine, EP. 130, 12, 22:PL 33, 503.
10 Cf. *Lk* 24:44.
11 Cf. Mt 5-7.
12 St. Thomas Aquinas, *STh* II-II, 83, 9.
13 Cf. *Jn* 17:7.
14 Cf. Mt 6:7; *1 Kings* 18:26-29.
15 *Jn* 6:63.
16 *Gal* 4:6.
17 *Rom* 8:27.
18 Cf. *Didache* 8, 3: SCh 248, 174.
19 St. John Chrysostom, *Hom. in Mt.* 19, 4: PG 57, 278.
20 *1 Pet* 1:23.
21 Cf. *1 Pet* 2:1-10.
22 *1 Jn* 3:2; cf. *Col* 3:4.
23 *1 Cor* 11:26.
24 Tertullian, *De orat.* 1:PL 1, 1251-1255.
25 St. Thomas Aquinas, *STH* II-II, 83, 9.
26 *Ex* 3:5.
27 *Heb* 1:3; 2:13.
28 St. Peter Chrysologus, *Sermo* 71,3: PL 52, 401CD; cf. *Gal* 4:6.
29 Cf. *Eph* 3:12; *Heb* 3:6; 4:16; 10:19; *1 Jn* 2:28; 3:21; 5:14.
30 Mt 11:25-27.
31 Tertullian, *De orat.* 3:PL 1,1155.
32 Cf. *Jn* 1:1; *1 Jn* 5:1.
33 Cf. *1 Jn* 1:3.
34 St. Cyril of Jerusalem, *Catech, myst.* 3, 1: PG 33, 1088A
35 St Cyprian, *De Dom. orat.* 9: PL 4, 525A.
36 Cf. GS 22 Sec. 1.
37 St. Ambrose, *De Sacr.* 5, 4, 19: PL 16:450-451.

38 St. Cyprian, *De Dom. orat.* 11: PL 4:526B.

39 St. John Chrysostom, *De orat Dom.* 3: PG 51,44.

40 St. *Gregory of Nyssa*, De orat. Dom. 2: PG 44, 1148B.

41 *Mt.* 18:3.

42 Cf. Mt 11:25.

43 St. John Casssian, *Coll.* 9, 18: PL 49, 788C.

44 St. Augustine, *De serm. Dom. in monte* 2, 4, 16: PL 34, 1276.

45 *Jn* 1:17; cf. *Hos* 2:21-22; 6:1-6.

46 *Rev* 21:7.

47 Cf. *1 Jn* 5:1; *Jn* 3:5.

48 *Rom* 8:29; cf. *Eph* 4:4-6.

49 *Acts* 4:32.

50 Cf. *UR* 8: 22.

51 Cf. *Mt* 5:23-24; 6:14-15.

52 Cf. *NA* 5.

53 *Jn* 11:52.

54 St. Augustine, *De serm. Dom. in monte* 2, 5, 18: PL 34, 1277.

55 St. Cyril of Jerusalem, *Catech, myst.* 5:11: PG 33, 1117.

56 Cf. *Gen* 3.

57 *Jer* 3:19-4:1a; *Lk* 15:18, 21.

58 Cf. *Isa* 45:8: *Ps* 85:12.

59 *Jn* 3:13; 12:32; 14:2-3; 16:28; 20:17; *Eph* 4:9-10; *Heb* 1:3; 2:13.

60 *Eph* 2:6; *Col* 3:3.

61 *2 Cor* 5:2; cf. *Phil* 3:20; *Heb* 13:14.

62 *Ad Diognetum* 5: PG 2, 1173.

63 *Ps* 42:7.

64 Cf. *Lk* 22:14; 12:50.

65 Cf. *1 Cor* 15:28.

66 Cf. *Ps* 111:9; *Lk* 1:49.

67 *Eph* 1:9,4.

68 Cf. *Ps* 8; *Isa* 6:3.

69 *Ps* 8:5; *Rom* 3:23; cf. *Gen* 1:26.

70 *Col* 3:10.

71 Cf. *Heb* 6:13.

72 *Ex* 15:1; cf. 3:14.

73 Cf. *Ex* 19:5-6.

74 *Ezek* 20:9, 14, 22, 39, cf. *Lev* 19:2.

75 Cf. *Mt* 1:21; *Lk* 1:31; *Jn* 8:28; 17:8; 17:17-19.

76 *Jn* 17:11,19.

77 Cf. *Ezek* 20:39; 36:20-21; *Jn* 17:6.

78 *Phil* 2:9-11.

79 *1 Cor* 6:11.

80 *1 Cor* 1:30; cf. *1 Thess* 4:7.

81 St. Cyprian, *De Dom. orat.* 12:PL 4, 527A; *Lev* 20:26.

82 St. Peter Chrysologus, *Sermo* 71, 4:PL 52:402A; cf. *Rom* 2:24; *Ezek* 36:20-22.

83 Tertullian, *De orat.* 3: PL 1:1157A.

84 Cf. *Jn* 14:13; 15:16; 16:24, 26.

85 *Jn* 17:11.

86 St. Cyprian, *De Dom. orat.* 13: PL 4, 528A.

87 Tertullian, *De orat.* 5: PL 1, 1159A; cf. *Heb* 4:11; *Rev* 6:9; 22:20.

88 Cf. *Titus* 2:13.

89 *Roman Missal*, Eucharistic Prayer IV, 118.

90 *Rom* 14:17.

91 Cf. *Gal* 5:16-25.

92 St. Cyril of Jerusalem, *Catech, myst.* 5, 13: PG 33, 1120A; cf. *Rom* 6:12.

93 Cf. *GS* 22; 32; 39; 45; *EN* 31.

94 Cf. *Jn* 17:17-20; *Mt* 5:13-16; 6:24; 7:12-13.

95 *1 Tim* 2:3-4.

96 *2 Pet* 3:9; cf. *Mt* 18:14.

97 *Jn* 13:34; cf. *1 Jn* 3; 4; *Lk* 10:25-37.

98 *Eph* 1:9-11.

99 *Heb* 10:7; *Ps* 40:7.

100 *Jn* 8:29.

101 *Lk* 22:42; cf. *Jn* 4:34; 5:30; 6:38.

102 *Gal* 1:4.

103 *Heb* 10:10.

104 *Heb* 5:8.

105 Cf. *Jn* 8:29.

106 Origen, *De orat.* 26:PG 11, 501B.

107 St. John Chrysostom, *Hom. in Mt.* 19, 5: PG 57, 280.

108 *Rom* 12:2; cf. *Eph* 5:17; cf. *Heb* 10:36.

109 *Mt* 7:21.

110 *Jn* 9:31; cf. *1 Jn* 5:14.

111 Cf *Lk* 1:38, 49.

112 St. Augustine, *De serm. Dom.* 2, 6, 24: PL 34, 1279.

113 *Mt* 5:45.

114 *Ps* 104:27.

115 Cf. *Mt* 6:25-34.

116 Cf. *2 Thess* 3:6-13.

117 St. Cyprian, De Dom. orat. 21: PL 4, 534A.

118 Cf. *Lk* 16:19-31; *Mt* 25-31-46.
119 Cf. *AA* 5.
120 Cf. *2 Cor* 8:1-15.
121 Cf. St. Benedict, *Regula*, 20, 48.
122 Attributed to St. Ignatius Loyola, cf. Joseph de Guibert, SJ, *The Jesuits: Their Spiritual Doctrine and Practice*, (Chicago: Loyola University Press, 1964), 148, n.55.
123 *Deut* 8:3; *Mt* 4:4.
124 *Am* 8:11.
125 Cf. *Jn* 6:26-58.
126 Cf. *Mt* 6:34, *Ex* 16:19.
127 St. Ambrose, *De Sacr.* 5, 4, 26: PL 16, 453A; cf. *Ps* 2:7.
128 Cf. *Ex* 16:19-21.
129 Cf. *1 Tim* 6:8.
130 St. Ignatius of Antioch, *Ad Eph.* 20, 2:PG 5, 661; *Jn* 6:53-56.
131 St. Augustine, *Sermo* 57, 7: PL 38, 389
132 St. Peter Chrysologus, Sermo 67, PL 52, 392; cf. *Jn* 6:51.
133 Cf. *Lk* 15:11-32; 18:13.
134 *Col* 1:14; *Eph* 1:7.
135 Cf. *Mt* 26:28; *Jn* 20:23.
136 Cf. *1 Jn* 4:20.
137 Cf. *Mt* 6:14-15; 5:23-24; *Mk* 11:25.
138 *Mt* 19:26.
139 *Mt* 5:48; *Lk* 6:36; *Jn* 13:34.
140 Cf. *Gal* 5:25; *Phil* 2:1,5.
141 *Eph* 4:32.
142 Cf. *Jn* 13:1.
143 Cf. *Mt* 18:23-35.
144 Cf. *Mt* 5:43-44.
145 Cf. *2 Cor* 5:18-21; John Paul II, *DM* 14.
146 Cf. *Mt* 18:21-22; *Lk* 17:3-4.
147 *Rom* 13:8
148 Cf. *Mt* 5:23-24; *1 Jn* 3:19-24.
149 St. Cyprian, *De Dom. orat.* 23: PL 4, 535-536; cf. *Mt* 5:24.
150 Cf. *Mt* 26:41.
151 *Jas* 1:13.
152 Cf. *Lk* 8:13-15; *Acts* 14:22; *Rom* 5:3-5; *2 Tim* 3:12.
153 Cf. *Jas* 1:14-15.
154 Cf. *Gen* 3:6.
155 Origen, *De orat.* 29: PG 11, 544CD.
156 *Mt* 6:21, 24.
157 *Gal* 5:25.
158 *1 Cor* 10:13.
159 Cf. *Mt* 4:1-11; 26:36-44.
160 *Jn* 17:11; cf. *Mk* 13:9, 23, 33-37; 14:38; *Lk* 12:35-40.
161 Cf. *1 Cor* 16:13; *Col* 4:2; *1 Thess* 5:6; *1 Pet* 5:8.
162 *Rev* 16:15.
163 *Jn* 17:15.
164 Cf. *RP* 16.
165 *Jn* 8:44; *Rev* 12:9.
166 *Roman Missal*, Eucharistic Prayer IV, 125.
167 *1 Jn* 5:18-19.
168 St. Ambrose, *De Sacr.* 5, 4, 30: PL 16, 454; cf. *Rom* 8:31.
169 *Jn* 14:30
170 *Jn* 12:31; *Rev* 12:10.
171 *Rev* 12:13-16.
172 *Rev* 12:17.
173 *Rev* 22:17,20.
174 *Rev* 1:8, 18; cf *Rev* 1:4; *Eph* 1:10.
175 *Roman Missal*, Embolism after the Lord's Prayer, 126.
176 Cf. *Rev* 1:6; 4:11; 5:13.
177 Cf. *Lk* 4:5-6.
178 *1 Cor* 15:24-28.
179 St. Cyril of Jerusalem, *Catech, myst.* 5, 18: PG 33, 1124; cf. Cf. *Lk* 1:38.

Make an Octave of Consecration to the Eternal Father

GOD OUR FATHER

CONSECRATION AND FEAST DAY FOR
THE FATHER OF ALL MANKIND

Inspired by the Holy Spirit, this beautiful, eight-day consecration prayer to the Eternal Father is something that all Catholics will find to be very special for enriching their faith. Consecration to God Our Father will certainly have a tremendous effect on those who practice this devotion and recite the daily chaplet.

Based entirely on Scriptural passages from both the Old and New Testament, this consecration prayer is founded on sound theology. A Chaplet of Consecration and Holy Octave Medal are also recommended to accompany this devotion.

This new devotion has been granted an Imprimatur.

GOD OUR FATHER

CONSECRATION AND FEAST DAY
FOR
THE FATHER OF ALL MANKIND

Only $1.99

Also Available!

The Holy Octave of Consecration to God Our Father Medal

Regular Medal:	$ 1.50
Large Medal:	$ 3.00
Small Chaplet	$ 5.00
Large Chaplet:	$15.00

Front　　　　**Back**

**ISBN:
1891903071**

Published By:

The Father of All Mankind Apostolate

Consecration Picture-Prayer Cards to God Our Father

Picture card:	$	.25ea.
4 x 6 with Litany:	$	.50ea.
10 x 16 no frame:	$	5.00ea.

Call for Quantity Discounts

Call Now! (412) 787-9735　Fax: (412) 787-5204　www.SaintAndrew.com

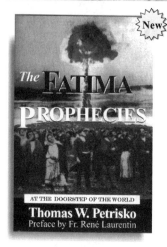
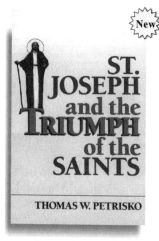

Listening to God
Ways of Hearing God's Voice
by Fr. Bill McCarthy, M.S.A.

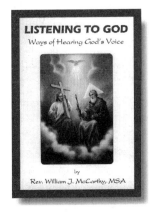

LISTENING TO GOD
Ways of Hearing God's Voice

by
Rev. William J. McCarthy, MSA

This beautifully illustrated prayer book outlines several sure fire methods for listening to the many ways God speaks to His people. Offering several principles for discerning God's voice both internally and externally, the practical suggestions in this book will teach readers how to enter into God's Will more deeply.   64 pages

Only $3.00

The Joy of Being Catholic
By Fr. Bill McCarthy, M.S.A.

Containing over 45 color illustrations and paintings, this wonderful prayer book tells of the countless joys of being Catholic. Covering the joy of the sacraments, the joy of a personal relationship with Jesus Christ, the joy of of Mary our mother, and the joy of being part of the Church founded by Jesus Christ, these beautiful writings and prayers will be sure to inspire all who read.   48 pages

Only $2.00

Call Now!   (412) 787-9735   Fax: (412) 787-5204   www.SaintAndrew.com

Order 'The Royal Bridegroom' Painting

'The Royal Bridegroom'
by Katie Burchfield

This beautiful painting portrays Jesus as the *Royal Bridegroom* who will one day come for His Bride, the Church. The painting is to give encouragement to God's children. It is also an invitation and wedding announcement. The arms of Jesus are opened wide showing His compassion to 'all.'

Order	Price	Qty.	Total
Prayer Card (laminated)	$ 1.00		
Bookmark (laminated)	$ 2.00		
5 1/2" x 7" poster	$ 3.00		
7 1/2" x 9" poster	$ 6.00		
15" x 18" poster	$15.00		
Royal Bridegroom Video	$12.00		

'The Alpha/Omega Cross'
(1" x 2" with chain)

This powerful, rotating crucifix portrays Jesus on one side as our Savior. The other side shows Christ as the Royal Bridegroom standing on the earth with the cross behind him.

Order	Price	Qty.	Total
Alpha/Omega Cross (1" x 2" with chain)	$20.00		
Rosary with Alpha/Omega Cross	$20.00		

| Make Checks Payable to:
Gisclar & Associates, Inc.
2970 Creek Park Drive
Marietta, GA 30062
(770) 973-0529
PGisclar@aol.com | **Shipping Cost**
Each Cross/
Poster
$2.50

Each Video
$4.00 | SUBTOTAL
SHIPPING
GA. TAX 6%
DONATION
TOTAL | |